Graphis Inc. is committed to presenting exceptional work in international Design, Advertising, Illustration & Photography.

Published by Graphis | Publisher & Creative Director: B. Martin Pedersen | Design: Ahhyun Rachel Kim
Editor: Annemarie McNamara | Production: Linh Truong | Executive Assistant: Sara Allen

Remarks: We extend our heartfelt thanks to contributors throughout the world who have made it possible to publish a wide and international spectrum of the best work in this field. Entry instructions for all Graphis Books may be requested from: Graphis Inc., 114 West 17th Street, Second Floor, New York, New York 10011, or visit our website at www.graphis.com.

Anmerkungen: Unser Dank gilt den Einsendern aus aller Welt, die es uns ermöglicht haben, ein breites, internationales. Spektrum der besten Arbeiten zu veröffentlichen. Teilnahmebedingungen für die Graphis-Bücher sind erhältlich bei: Graphis, Inc., 114 West 17th Street, Second Floor, New York, New York 10011. Besuchen Sie uns im World Wide Web, www.graphis.com.

Remerciements: Nous remercions les participants du monde entier qui ont rendu possible la publication de cet ouvrage offrant un panorama complet des meilleurs travaux. Les modalités d'inscription peuvent être obtenues auprès de: Graphis, Inc., 114 West 17th Street, Second Floor, New York, New York 10011. Rendez-nous visite sur notre site web: www.graphis.com.

Contents

InMemoriam

Bob Brooks
Advertising Art Director
1928–2012

Russ Alben
Advertising Executive
1930–2012

Stephen Frankfurt
Pioneer in Advertising
1931–2012

G. William Ruhl
Advertising Executive
1939–2012

Originally from Michigan, Brad Emmett now resides in New York City. Upon graduating from NYC's School of Visual Arts, he began his career at DeVito/Verdi. There, he won numerous major awards, including the coveted One Show Pencil and a Cannes Lion for his work on National Thoroughbred Racing. After eight years at DeVito/Verdi, he moved on to BBDO, where he worked on brands such as FedEx, Pepsi, and GE. He went on to be Creative Director at Cliff Freeman and Partners. While at Cliff Freeman, Brad's award-winning creative work continued, with accolades for his efforts on behalf of Snapple, CBS, Sports Authority, and the Youth AIDS Awareness project. He then returned to the place it all started, DeVito/Verdi, where he is currently Creative Director. Beyond his many accomplishments in the field, Brad is also a co-founder of the advertising school called 101theadschool.com. He is the writer and co-creator of the Learn Just Enough to Get Laid series, which is a book/trans-media property that aims to help guys learn a fair amount of a variety of skills to get an entirely different job accomplished. TBS recently purchased the book, and is developing it into a sitcom. Brad's claimed proof that his method works? He married a Radio City Rockette.

Your entry states that Daffy's fashion sales increased by double digits during the period the campaign ran. Were there other successes? Did you receive other comments about the campaign?
Creatively, this campaign was well liked throughout the industry, but the biggest success was getting people in the door, period. Daffy's main problem was that consumers thought of Daffy's as a discount retailer, but not a fashion discount retailer. If you were to ask anyone where to get fashions for less in New York City, Daffy's would never be on a respectable fashionista's radar until this campaign launched. With a limited budget we were able to compete with H&M, TJ Maxx, and many discounters, or at least those the fashionista bloggers had started to blog about.

Can you speak about this campaign's use of humor as a focal point?
Oftentimes fashion advertising takes itself too seriously, much to the amusement of consumers. That inspired us to focus on the unintentional humor of fashion advertising.

Brad Emmett
Creative Director

The odd thing here is her $850 heels are just $189.

DAFFY'S

I met Sal Devito when I was nineteen at SVA. His first words to me were, "What are you going to do for a living? Because you won't make it in advertising." After that I set out to prove him wrong.

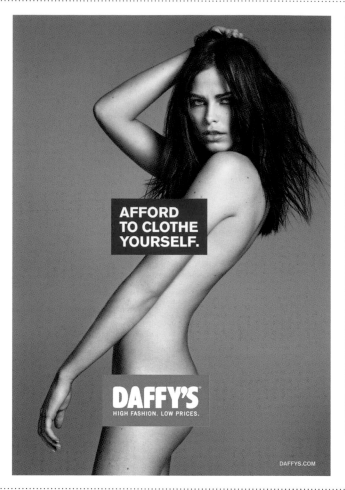

What caused you to take a step further than conventional campaigns with this one?

After doing Daffy's advertising for ten or more years, Daffy's left DeVito/Verdi and went to another agency that gave them conventional advertising. When convention didn't work, they came back to us and said, "We need to get people in the doors. Do what you think is right for the brand."

What is your creative philosophy, if you have one?

What I enjoy most is smart, funny work. I always lead with smart, though, because funny is subjective. Combining the two successfully is a win.

What inspires you in your work?

Truth! Truth inspires me. I believe you don't have to make anything up for an ad. There is enough reality in our lives to steal from.

What and who are some of your influences?

My biggest influence by far is Sal DeVito. He changed the way I think and how I approach advertising. I met Sal Devito when I was nineteen at The School of Visual Arts. The first words he said to me were, "What are you going to do for a living? Because you won't make it in advertising." After that I set out to prove him wrong.

Who do you most admire in your profession, past or present, and why?

I know you expect me to give a creative's name, but who I most admire are the clients who are willing to take risks. It's so easy for a client to do something safe that they will never have to answer for. I tell the clients to save their money if they want to do something safe, because nobody is going to pay attention to their advertising if they are safe and boring. Oh, but I also admire Eric Silver, Jerry Graff, Ian Reichenthal, and Scott Vitrone. Even though I haven't directly worked for them, I've learned a lot from them.

How do you feel this campaign connected with its viewers?

If nothing else, the Daffy's campaign was interesting. It was designed to stop people as they were walking throughout New York. An ad is supposed to stop a consumer, but if you stop a consumer with nothing interesting to say, then you have probably pissed them off. You don't want to piss off a consumer, especially a New York City consumer.

What might be your dream campaign (in general or specific)? What are you aiming for in coming campaigns?

I think my dream campaign is one that makes the client happy, as well as the award shelves sag. I want to do a campaign that sticks in the consumer's head, like "Just do it" does, not like "We wear short shorts" did. Every year someone does a campaign that makes all creatives say, "I wish I did that." That is the response I always shoot for when starting a new project.

How do you see the advertising world changing?

Of course, the media space has changed a lot since I got into advertising, but what is still true to any good agency is that a great idea is a great idea no matter where it's showcased.

What media are you doing more of? (For example, are you doing more Internet and mobile work?)

Like most agencies, DeVito/Verdi has transitioned into an agency that does digital as well as traditional. Speaking in percentages, we are 40% digital and 60% traditional. All of our clients want digital, but in actuality haven't budgeted properly to execute some of the digital ideas. To answer your question, we do more traditional with some client hand-holding into the digital space.

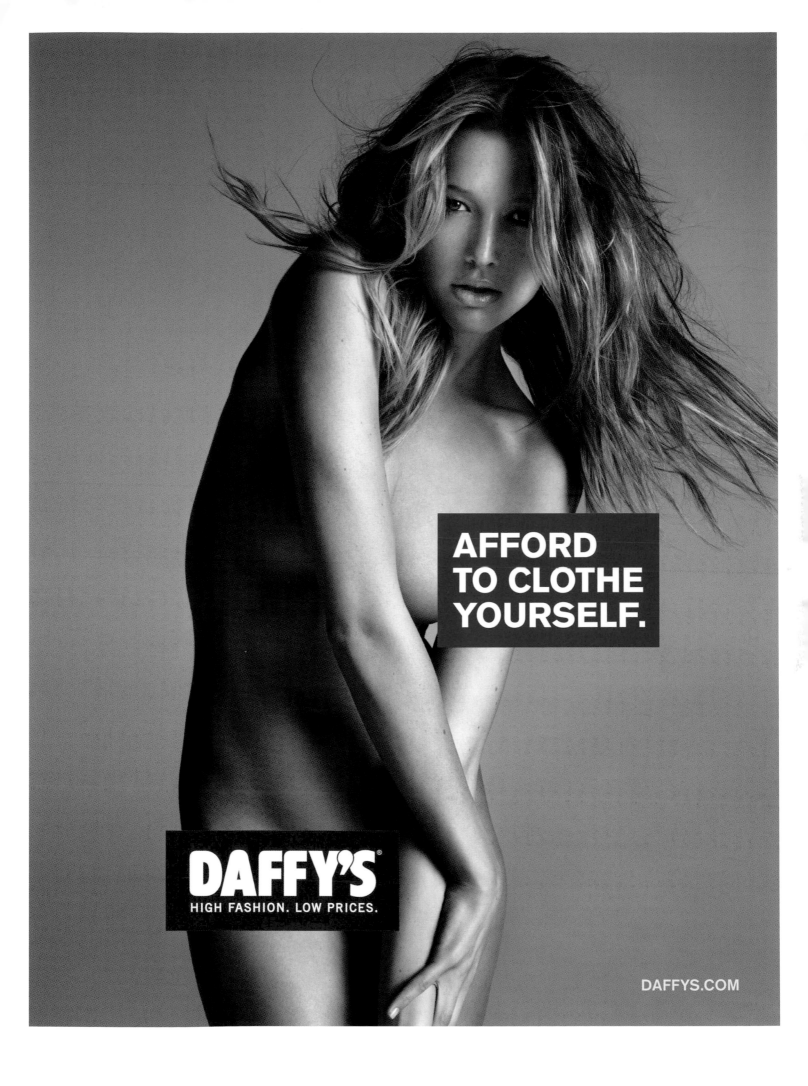

AFFORD
TO CLOTHE
YOURSELF.

DAFFY'S®
HIGH FASHION. LOW PRICES.

DAFFYS.COM

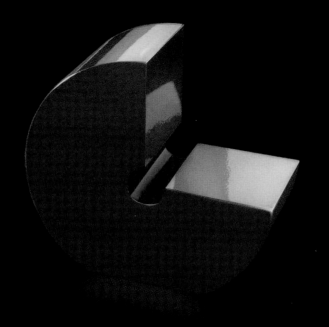

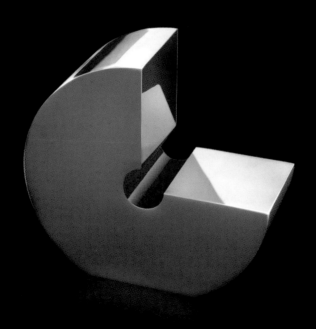

Innocean Worldwide Americas Creative Director: Robert Prins **Client: Hyundai** P. 24

Mcgarrybowen Creative Directors: Howie Ronay, Gerald Cuesta, Mary Knight, Todd Tilford **Client: Motorola** P. 70

LLOYD&CO Creative Directors: Doug Lloyd, Jason Evans **Client: Oscar de la Renta** P. 108

Publicis/New York Creative Directors: Rob Feakins, David Corr, Scott Davis **Client: P&G/Scope** P. 44

DeVito/Verdi Creative Director: Brad Emmett **Client: Daffy's** P. 210

Saatchi & Saatchi, New York Creative Directors: Aaron Alamo, Joseph Pompeo **Client: Novartis Lamisil** P. 128

Après anything. **SOREL**

sorel.com

Butler, Shine, Stern & Partners Executive Creative Director: Mike Shine **Client: Sorel** P. 102

Advertising Agency: Butler, Shine, Stern & Partners   **Art Director:** Sinan Dagli   **Client:** MINI USA

Creative Director: Steve Mapp, Lyle Yetman   **Copywriter:** Bem Jimmerson

ASSIGNMENT

Situation: Develop a campaign to address an automatic inventory issue, while also seeding the idea and exhilaration of driving a manual.

Business Goal: Increase the manual transmission preference/take rates across R5X and R60 models to address the abundance of manual inventory.

Marketing Problem: Conquest shoppers in-market for a manual transmission. Get MINI on their shopping list. Convert "Automatics" at the dealership. Demonstrate how a manual should be considered.

APPROACH

Materials developed for the campaign included video content, display banners, rich media units, and print.

Strategy: Seed the idea of manual through targeted digital media and social media channels.

Provide showroom and marketing materials to dealerships to help sell the benefits of manual driving by appealing to the consumer's inner driving enthusiast.

Utilize existing auto shopping sites to reach in-market shoppers (KBB, Cars.com, Yahoo Auto, etc.).

Use highly targeted lifestyle sites or auto enthusiast sites.

RESULTS

Take rate of over 3,000 for $500 Manual incentive in August/September.

Manual Sales up 19% YOY in September and up 30% YOY in October.

128 million online impressions, over 50,000 engagement clicks, and almost 13,000 views of Manualhood Video on YouTube.

Positive press from *Marketing Daily, AdWeek*, and *Motortrend*.

Positive feedback from dealers and a wide use of materials for local campaigns.

BUY TWO PEDALS, GET ONE FREE.

 MANUAL

At MINI, we think it's time to manual up. Why? More control. Better gas mileage. More pure motoring exhilaration, that's why. Yes, it might take a little getting used to. But darn it, it's worth it. Because if you're not already, we're gonna make a manual out of you yet.

Advertising Agency: Butler, Shine, Stern and Partners	**Art Director:** John Verrochi
Creative Director: Steve Mapp, Lyle Yetman	**Copywriter:** Chris Bull **Client:** MINI USA

ASSIGNMENT

When we were given the opportunity to produce an ad specifically for the small issue of *Dwell* magazine, we decided to speak to interior design enthusiasts in their own language.

APPROACH

The resulting ad invited drivers to sample the new MINI Coupe's road-holding ability on a variety of surfaces with names that we hope are as evocative as any from Sherwin-Williams.

Interstate Slate
423

Pure Pavement
008

Full-Throttle Flint
403

Basic Byway
901

Truly Turnpike
281

Dusty Trail
324

Expressway Gray
471

Absolute Asphalt
416

Off-Ramp Obsidian
870

Regal Roadway
1058

Tennessee Tarmac
409

DESIGNED FOR THE ROAD.

THE NEW MINI COUPE. HOLD ON.

MINIUSA.COM

Advertising Agency: Charit Art Co., Ltd.   **Creative Director:** Charit Pusiri   **Client:** Toyota Motor Thailand Co., Ltd.

ASSIGNMENT

This assignment was to create an ad for the Toyota Prius in Thailand. As it is one of the first hybrid cars to be sold in Thailand, the client would like to focus on its hybrid features. The goal was to show the audience the characteristics of this hybrid car in a creative, fun, and unconventional way.

APPROACH

After analyzing the product, we found its prominent characteristics are that it's energy saving, clean, quiet, and easy to drive. Then we decided to emphasize the cleanness and the quietness of the car.

To link the cleanness characteristic with the goal of being unconventional, we came up with an idea of parking the car in a bedroom, which people normally perceive as a clean place and also an unconventional place to park a car. The scenario of a couple in the bedroom became the answer of how to visualize the car's prominent characteristics of being clean and quiet. The wife is sleeping without any worries, thinking that if her licentious husband goes out in the middle of the night, she will hear the noise of the car parked next to her when it starts. Unfortunately, she underestimates the car, and her husband successfully escapes. This scenario aims to represent the quiet and clean characteristics of the car in a fun and interesting way.

RESULTS

The client loved the idea, because it is very easy to understand, fun, and creative, and it makes their product seem more interesting and not focused too much on energy savings, which can be boring sometimes. With its humor and unconventionality, the ad could also make the younger generation interested in their product.

Advertising Agency: Innocean Worldwide Americas   **Art Director:** Frauke Tiemann

Creative Director: Robert Prins   **Copywriter:** Kevin Samuels   **Client:** Hyundai

ASSIGNMENT

The Hyundai Veloster is a new kind of car. One that has all the technology and connectivity of a handheld device, wrapped in a cool and stylish package the likes of nothing Generation Y has ever seen. Our assignment was to get the word out that this fun car has arrived.

APPROACH

Each ad in this campaign was designed to focus on one cool feature of the Veloster, and present it in a simple and stylish graphic way that would stop a magazine reader in his tracks.

RESULTS

The Veloster has gained a tremendous amount of great automotive press, as well as a little bit of a cult following. And sales have been great in all age groups.

Finding super-fresh sushi or the best burger in town is fast and delicious in the Veloster, thanks to Blue Link™ technology with Restaurant Ratings. YouTube.com/VELOSTER. **Engineered for whatever.**

ÜBER DRIVE.

When you're not playing Xbox 360® or watching movies on the 7-inch touchscreen of the Veloster, you can always upload your favorite photos to its hard drive. YouTube.com/VELOSTER. **Engineered for whatever.**

Advertising Agency: Innocean Worldwide Americas **Art Director:** Tom Gibson **Copywriter:** Steve O'Brien

Creative Directors: Robert Prins, Doug James **Client:** Hyundai

ASSIGNMENT

Our goal was to greater awareness of the Hyundai Genesis rising higher up in the performance food chain with the addition of the R-Spec model. With 429 hp, 8 speeds, and a 5.0L V8 engine that goes 0–60 in 4.8 seconds, the Genesis R-Spec is a true luxury performance vehicle.

APPROACH

The Facebook "Like" button—an instantly recognized, shared cultural reference—seemed a natural way to connect the Genesis R-Spec with performance. At the time, it hadn't been used in an advertisement, so being first to appropriate it was also a consideration.

RESULTS

The ad created greater awareness of Hyundai's offering more luxury performance vehicles.
The Genesis also went on to be ranked by J.D. Power as "The Most Dependable Midsize Premium Car."

Advertising Agency: Innocean Worldwide Americas

Art Directors: Tyson Brown, Joe Reynoso

Creative Director: Ed Miller

Copywriters: Shawn Wood, Cooper Olson

Client: Hyundai

ASSIGNMENT

This project took the fact that Hyundai had been named #1 in customer loyalty and marketed that fact to some of the most loyal people on the planet, college football fans. The goal was to take Hyundai's commitment to its products and its customers' commitment to their cars and equate it to college football fans' commitment to their teams.

APPROACH

To demonstrate the kind of devotion it takes to be #1 in customer loyalty, we found extreme examples of the lengths to which people would go to show their loyalty to a particular team. In this case, we photographed the Sod Cemetery at Florida State University. Buried in this hallowed ground is a piece of turf from every significant FSU road victory since 1962. A monument with the opponent, score, and date marks each grave. Many photographs at many times of the day were taken until the perfect moment was found to capture this symbol of loyalty.

FLORIDA STATE UNIVERSITY. THE SOD CEMETERY.

#1 IN CUSTOMER LOYALTY.

There are no words to accurately describe true loyalty. It runs too deep. Touches places in us that even memory can't reach. Where we are both our strongest and most vulnerable. So, instead, we use examples to describe our loyalty. Analogies. Anecdotes. Stories that, as they're told over and over, by more and more people, become something more indelible than even the truth. They become tradition. To be reenacted and retold by the next generation. Followed by the next. And the next. And the next.

Hyundai.com

HYUNDAI | NEW THINKING NEW POSSIBILITIES.

Advertising Agency: Innocean Worldwide Americas   **Art Director:** Arnie Presiado   **Creative Director:** Robert Prins

Copywriter: Jeb Quaid   **Client:** Hyundai

ASSIGNMENT

When it comes to luxury cars most people don't think of Hyundai, but the Equus is a true luxury car in every aspect. It competes easily with Lexus and Mercedes, and features most of the same attributes that make those cars a premium purchase. The only difference is the price; the Equus is a lot less expensive. Hoity: You get all the luxury and performance. Not Toity: You don't pay the premium price.

APPROACH

Educate consumers about this new entry into the luxury car market. Use wit and confidence to create a new reality for the brand Hyundai as a true luxury competitor.

RESULTS

In addition to many favorable reviews and enthusiastic press, sales goals continue to be met every month since the Equus debut.

HOITY.
NOT TOITY.

Discover luxury without pretention at HyundaiEquus.com.

 HYUNDAI | NEW THINKING.
NEW POSSIBILITIES.

Advertising Agency: Goodby, Silverstein & Partners **Art Director:** Raphael Milcarek **Producer:** Jim King

Copywriter: Matt Lanzdorf **Executive Creative Directors:** Hunter Hindman, Rick Condos

Photographer: Anatol Kotte **Client:** Chevrolet

HUMBLE *is for pie.*

The new 426-horsepower Camaro SS Convertible is here. **Chevy Runs Deep**

Advertising Agency: Butler, Shine, Stern & Partners

Art Director: John Verrochi

Creative Directors: Steve Mapp, Lyle Yetman

Copywriter: Chris Bull

Client: MINI USA

ASSIGNMENT

Use the Coupe launch as an opportunity for MINI to rekindle the passions of the original MINI enthusiasts, who might be looking elsewhere, and to inspire a new generation of MINI enthusiasts.

APPROACH

The Coupe—positioned as a fun-to-drive, fast, performance car—called for a stunt that reinforced this notion in a clever way. When the time came to launch the car, we took the notion of "launch" a little more literally than usual, creating a full-scale rocket with a Coupe attached to it, smoking jetboosters and all. The rocket launch concept was the centerpiece of the Chelsea Triangle in New York City, complete with street teams of roving astronauts, space ice-cream giveaways, Foursquare check-ins, moonwalk competitions, and more.

RESULTS

The live stunt, located in the Meatpacking District at 14th and 9th Streets in New York City from October 27th through November 1st, reached 90,000 spectators daily.

The Coupe Rocket was a stop along the NYC Halloween Parade, which was attended by over 2 million people.

Facebook and Twitter reach exceeded 6MM.

The results were memorable, impactful, and left no one in doubt about the car's performance. Client reactions were excited and positive. This stunt created buzz beyond the general stunt area.

PREPARE FOR LAUNCH.
THE NEW MINI COUPE. HOLD ON.

PREPARE FOR LAUNCH.
THE NEW MINI COUPE. HOLD ON.

Consult a physician before motoring if you:

1. Suffer from motorphobia
2. Are allergic to fun
3. Have acceleration deficit disorder
4. Just ate a huge lunch
5. Have adrenaline intolerance
6. Are velocity-averse
7. Wear false teeth
8. Don't like the idea of being strapped to a rocket

THE NEW MINI COUPE. HOLD ON.

MINI COUPE
ICE CREAM.

THE NEW MINI COUPE.
HOLD ON.

Creating buzz for a new model from MINI isn't exactly rocket science, except when it is. When the time came to introduce the new MINI Coupe to America we took the notion of a product launch a little more literally than usual, creating a full scale rocket to grace the streets of New York as the centerpiece of our campaign. Other campaign elements expanded on the space them including a street team decked out in spacesuits. The results were memorable, impactful and left no one in doubt about the car's performance.

Advertising Agency: pp+k   **Art Director:** Kris Gregoire   **Associate Creative Director:** Michael Schillig

Copywriter: Michael Schillig   **Executive Creative Director:** Tom Kenney   **Client:** Tires Plus

ASSIGNMENT

According to AAA, 70% of the cars on the road today need an alignment. Our assignment was to capitalize on this opportunity and create awareness for a Straight-Forward Alignment service offered by Tires Plus. They had always provided this service, but they wanted to brand it and communicate it in a bold, new way. Ultimately, Tires Plus hoped to increase their number of alignment services and generate additional revenue.

APPROACH

In order to really capture consumers' attention and promote the Straight-Forward Alignment service offered by Tires Plus, we decided to create a floor graphic that would be placed at the outside entrance of their stores. Since potholes were one of the biggest causes for throwing cars out of alignment, we decided to create a "monster" pothole, complete with jagged rocks for teeth. Through this dramatic visual, we would immediately capture a consumer's attention, so that they might inquire further about having an alignment done, especially if they recently ran over a big pothole or other road hazard.

RESULTS

Through this powerful, visually driven floor graphic, we were able to generate new inquiries from customers about Tires Plus's Straight-Forward Alignment service and ultimately increase the amount of alignment checks at Tires Plus. It served as a good conversation starter, and gave their associates the opportunity to further emphasize the advantages of having your car properly aligned to improve its ride and save on gas.

SWALLOWED BY A MONSTROUS POTHOLE? ASK ABOUT OUR STRAIGHT-FORWARD ALIGNMENT SERVICE

This floor graphic was placed at the outside entrance of all Pinellas County Tires Plus stores and was designed to promote their newly branded Straight-Forward Alignment service.

Advertising Agency: pp+k   **Art Director:** Trushar Patel   **Associate Creative Director:** Michael Schillig

Copywriter: Michael Schillig   **Executive Creative Director:** Tom Kenney   **Client:** Tires Plus

ASSIGNMENT

Our assignment was to create a poster that would commemorate the historic grand opening of a new Tires Plus store in West Palm Beach, Florida. This was no ordinary grand opening, because it marked the 2,200th new store opening in their organization's illustrious history. We wanted to communicate this in a big, bold way at the new store's grand opening event, so everybody would know how the company is expanding in spite of the stagnate economy.

APPROACH

We set out to design a commemorative in-store poster for the grand opening day celebration that would really stand out and best sum up the company's strong growth and expansion over the years. With this in mind, we came up with a distinctive way to convey this impressive number of store openings by literally including every number (from 1 to 2,200) and creating a tire out of these highlighted numerals. When viewed from a distance, the tire created out of numbers becomes vividly revealed and really captures people's attention.

RESULTS

This memorable poster was well received by Tires Plus and all those individuals who saw it at the grand opening celebration. It elicited lots of positive reactions for its unique and innovative design. The poster also served as a nice commemorative icon that reinforced the company's growth, and it still hangs in the store today.

WE HAVE A NUMBER OF REASONS TO CELEBRATE

as we proudly commemorate the grand opening of our organization's 2,200th store on May 11-13, 2012. Together we will continue to grow and accomplish great things down the road.

1905 NORTH JOG ROAD, WEST PALM BEACH, FL 33411

Advertising Agency: Publicis, New York   **Chief Creative Officer:** Rob Feakins   **Excutive Creative Director:** David Corr

Copywriter: Larissa Kirschner   **Creative Director:** Scott Davis   **Art Buyer:** Darielle Smolian

Client: P&G/Scope

ASSIGNMENT

Bad breath is an invisible villain—never seen, yet incredibly vicious. Our challenge was to personify it in a way that has never been done.

APPROACH

If bad breath had a shape, what would it be? Who would it be? We wanted to use humor to illustrate this in an unexpected way that was visually arresting.

RESULTS

The print ads were designed to build awareness of the problem without any specific performance indicators, call to action, or results matrix.

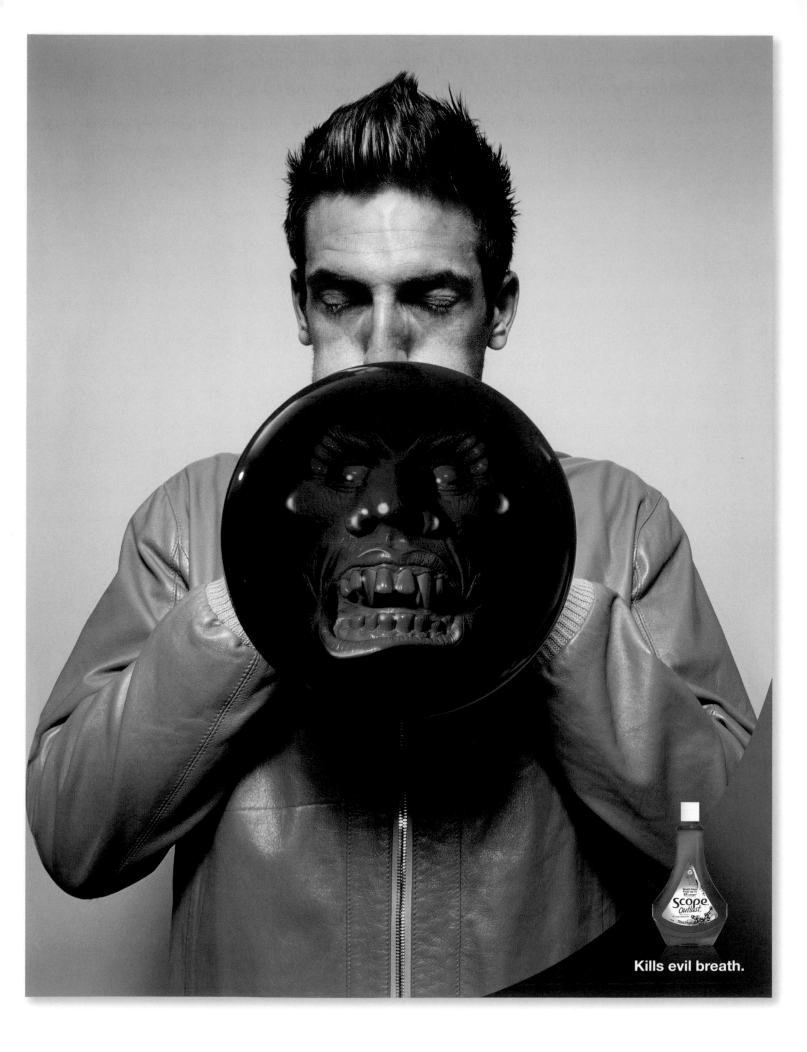

Kills evil breath.

Kills evil breath.

Advertising Agency: Hakuhodo, Inc. **Client:** Kanebo, Inc.

Creative Directors: Howard Schatz, Shigeaki Matsubara, Eriko Hoashi, Nobuyuki Miyadera

ASSIGNMENT

I made this image underwater for a campaign for a skin-care product. The goal was to communicate the feeling of silky smoothness.

APPROACH

There is a magical unpredictability, almost always filled with surprise and amazement, when working underwater—the weightlessness—as if slowly gliding in the air. One can hear the music, and feel a dream.

RESULTS

This has been an enormously successful campaign. It has been renewed with fresh images and expanded into world-wide territory since its first iteration.

SENSAI

Kanebo
INTERNATIONAL

Advertising Agency: beacon communications k.k.

Executive Creative Directors: Masahiko Yasuda, Jon King

Creative Director: Keizo Mugita

Associate Creative Director: Minoru Hongo

Art Directors: Tomo Tanaka, Hisamichi Takase

Client: P&G

ASSIGNMENT

The brief was very simple: to help Japanese consumers better understand the benefit of the Oral B electric toothbrush (3D rotating round) that cleans hidden plaque between teeth.

APPROACH

Japan is a very electric appliance savvy country; however, electric toothbrush consideration is very low, as most consumers don't really know why they need electric. We had this insight that people are most concerned about the cleanliness of their teeth after meals or long stints of travel. Then we realized how perfectly an airport baggage carousel resembled teeth. All baggage carousels have straight and curved areas, and the separate pieces get bigger around the corners. This perfectly represented our objective of revealing the "hidden," and is how the design comes to life.

RESULTS

We put QR codes on the carousels. QR codes have a very high usage rate in Japan; they have been around for over ten years here and are a common tool to jump online. So the QR codes gave consumers a chance to win a product, and if they didn't win, they were encouraged to go to any one of the consumer electronic stores in the surrounding area. During the campaign time the client saw sales increase by 127%.

Advertising Agency: YARD   **Creative Director:** Stephen Niedzwiecki   **Client:** John Varvatos Star USA

ASSIGNMENT

This John Varvatos Star USA project challenged YARD to translate the Star USA tier for fragrance licensee Elizabeth Arden, using arresting and unexpected advertising, while staying true to YARD's innovative approach to branding the John Varvatos portfolio.

APPROACH

For the Star USA fragrance project, YARD articulated a brand muse—"the artistically rebellious visionary who is not a wannabe but an about to be"—which inspired the creation of the innovative fragrance bottle and its campaign. The concept, a six-fingered peace sign, was designed to evoke this artistically rebellious muse. This subtle twist on the iconic Star USA imagery effectively communicates the brand's smart, irreverent spirit.

RESULTS

John Varvatos Star USA fragrance was awarded the prestigious 2012 Fifi for Best Men's Luxe Packaging.

JOHN VARVATOS ★ U.S.A.

THE NEW FRAGRANCE FOR YOUR SIXTH SENSE

johnvarvatos.com

Advertising Agency: HOOK **Art Directo:** Brady Waggoner **Designers:** Trish Ward, Andrew Smock

Copywriter: Tom Jeffrey **Photographer:** Jason Kaumeyer **Client:** Charleston Mix

ASSIGNMENT

Design a logo. Design the package. Build a set of lead creative that can be used in every type of tactical element. Differentiate the brand from less sophisticated, mass produced products. Ultimately help widen the product's footprint in the country.

APPROACH

Charleston Mix is delicious. It has tons of ingredients. Bloody Mary drinkers are a special group of people. They are experienced and love flavors. We aimed to show the world what the ultimate Charlestonian Bloody Mary snobs would look like and how they would talk. We figured they may even be opinionated people that don't look very nice. So they all have an injury to show that they like to have a good time—maybe even do some things they don't mention to Momma. We also needed to develop some trade and promotional items. Most Charlestonians overdress. The Blazer T is something we had never seen before, so the idea worked well to make a pleasantly disruptive statement for the brand.

RESULTS

Charleston Mix has been featured on FOX News, won "Best of the South" in *Garden & Gun Magazine,* and has vastly expanded distribution. Our favorite part is what the company had to say about the first mockup of the Blazer T. The owner said, "It's amazing. I bet this is what was in the suitcase in Pulp Fiction."

BOLD & SPICY. LIKE LAST NIGHT.

BLOODY MARY MIX. PERFECTED WITH NATURAL INGREDIENTS.
ENJOY EVERY SIP. CHARLESTONMIX.COM

IT'S EASY TO GRIN WHEN YOUR SHIP COMES IN.

BLOODY MARY MIX. PERFECTED WITH NATURAL INGREDIENTS.
ENJOY EVERY SIP. CHARLESTONMIX.COM

Advertising Agency: GSD&M   **Art Director:** Matt Barker   **Group Creative Director:** Luke Sullivan

Creative Directors: Jeff Maki, Robert Lin   **Writer:** Colin Gray   **Illustrator:** Federico Archuleta

Associate Creative Director: Ryan Carroll   **Client:** Jarritos

ASSIGNMENT

Our goal with the "We're Not From Here" campaign was to increase awareness of Jarritos Mexican soda among 18- to 24-year-olds in the general market, with an entertaining campaign that rewarded discovery. While Jarritos sodas are getting easier to find, they aren't easy to open. So we created posters that capture the brand's Mexican heritage, with a bottle opener built right in.

APPROACH

We decided to embrace the product's key attributes up front: Jarritos sodas come in glass bottles without a twist-off top. The posters reinforce brand awareness and identity, while also providing a helpful service—getting the cap off so consumers can enjoy the soda. We also partnered with food trucks in Los Angeles and Austin to put the product into many more consumers' hands.

RESULTS

By choosing popular and up-and-coming food trucks to partner with, we were able to significantly increase brand awareness among our target demographic.

Advertising Agency: Pentagram Design   **Art Director:** Michael Gericke   **Designers:** Michael Gericke, Matt McInerny, Kelly Sung

Client: Rockefeller Foundation

ASSIGNMENT

Create a bold and elegant new advertising campaign and graphic program for Top of the Rock that highlights the amazing, one-of-a-kind vistas seen from its observation deck.

APPROACH

To capture the unique Top of the Rock experience, Pentagram developed an unusual treatment of the skyline that transcends familiar images of the city. The views at Top of the Rock change continuously throughout the days and seasons, and the campaign pieces together a panoramic assemblage of images taken from the observation deck from day to night. Specific views—looking north, looking south, and so on—are assembled from multiple images, showcasing the spectacular all-around vista from the deck, as well as suggesting the many points of view available to visitors. The iconic photographic treatment has been paired with a memorable tagline, "Any Point of View." An integral element of the campaign, the tagline highlights the unobstructed views and has an embedded double meaning. The "NY" in "Any" has been set in bold to provide another read—"A NY Point of View"—that emphasizes Top of the Rock as a one-of-a-kind New York experience.

RESULTS

Following the launch of the campaign, the Top of the Rock has experienced significant increase in attendance, awareness, and visibility across many forms of media.

ANY POINT OF VIEW™

TOP
OF THE
ROCK®

Observation Deck at Rockefeller Center®
50th Street Between 5th and 6th Avenue
Open Daily from 8am to Midnight
212–698-2000 | topoftherocknyc.com

Advertising Agency: Mcgarrybowen

Creative Directors and Art Directors: Michael McGrath, Howie Ronay

Copywriter: Laura Keeler

Creative Director: Gerald Cuesta

Group Creative Director: Mary Knight

Client: Motorola

Chief Creative Officer: Todd Tilford

56 COMPUTERS GOLD MOTOROLA MOTOACTV - FULL BODY

ONE PERFORMANCE INSPIRES ANOTHER.
Introducing MOTO**ACTV**™ The GPS fitness tracker that intuitively uses music
to push you to new levels of athletic performance. **LIFE.** POWERED.
motoactv.com

ONE PERFORMANCE INSPIRES ANOTHER.
Introducing MOTO**ACTV**™ The GPS fitness tracker that intuitively uses music
to push you to new levels of athletic performance. **LIFE.** POWERED.
motoactv.com

Advertising Agency: John McNeil Studio   **Executive Creative Director:** Kim Le Liboux   **Art Director:** Per Nilsson

Creative Director, Senior Copywriter: Peter Rudy   **Client:** Juniper Networks

ASSIGNMENT

Created as part of the "Defend Your Mobile Life" campaign for Juniper Networks, this was a co-branded ad between Samsung and Juniper, intended to target the growing trend of "B.Y.O.D." (bring your own device) in the workplace. Consumers want to use one device in both their personal and work lives, but for I.T. pros, this poses enormous security risks. The Junos Pulse security application solves this problem easily for I.T.

APPROACH

We tapped into both the demand on the employee side and the solution on the I.T. side with a simple, clever headline: "Angry Birds. Happy I.T."

RESULTS

"Angry Birds," along with the other ads in the campaign, was instrumental in creating a platform for both Samsung and Juniper to market to the BtoB mobile audience in a way that was both engaging and relevant. The ad was very well received by both Juniper and Samsung.

ANGRY BIRDS.
HAPPY I.T.

Introducing the Galaxy Note. Combined with Junos® Pulse mobile security software, it's the perfect work phone for people who still like to play. Learn more at **juniper.net/samsung**

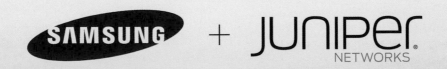

Advertising Agency: MRM/McCann - Salt Lake	Executive Creative Director: Brian Deaver	Client: Intel
Group Creative Director: Jeff Paris	Associate Creative Director: Ann Ford	Photographer: Josh Wood

ASSIGNMENT

Create a print and online campaign to promote Ultrabook to consumers, while connecting the devices to the consumer passion points of food, music, and sports. We also wanted them to know Ultrabooks are powered by Intel, our client.

APPROACH

Sleek design is what defines an Ultrabook. We developed a concept that would show off just how thin and sexy these machines are, in a way that engages the audience and encourages them to spot the Ultrabook in each ad.

RESULTS

Testing showed our ads significantly increased Ultrabook attribution to Intel and exceeded norms in likability and relevance, a wonky way of saying they worked great. One of the ads was posted on Intel's Facebook page, where it garnered over 30,000 Likes and more than 3,000 Shares. Plus, the campaign got shout-outs from various blogs.

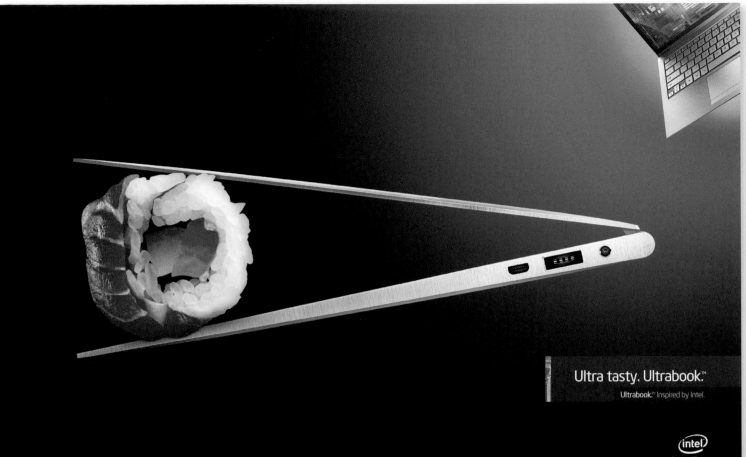

Ultra tasty. Ultrabook.™

Ultrabook.™ Inspired by Intel.

Ultra spin. Ultrabook.™

Ultrabook.™ Inspired by Intel.

Advertising Agency: mcgarrybowen

Creative Director and Art Director: Howie Ronay

Copywriter: Gerald Cuesta

Creative Director: Gerald Cuesta

Group Creative Director: Mary Knight

Client: Motorola

Chief Creative Officer: Todd Tilford

Advertising Agency: MiresBall   **Creative Director:** John Ball   **Designer:** Angela Renac

Copywriter: Brian Ellstrom   **Photographer:** Marc Tule   **Account Supervisor:** Bob Zucco

Client: Intel

ASSIGNMENT

Get opinion leaders to think of Intel as more than a PC-focused company.

APPROACH

We developed a series of ads highlighting areas of innovation not usually associated with Intel to show how the company is helping produce real, tangible advances in everyday experiences, such as healthcare, transportation, energy, and education. Multiple and consecutive ad placements helped paint the larger picture of all the ways Intel is creating technologies that reach far beyond PCs and servers. The integrated campaign also included digital out-of-home and radio.

RESULTS

Intel research confirmed the campaign was well received by target audiences, who consistently noted the ads boosted their impression of Intel as a visionary technology leader, beyond just processors or PCs.

Sponsors of:

HEAD-TO-TOE HEALTHCARE AT YOUR FINGERTIPS.

Diagnostic tools that send data directly to physicians. Devices that let doctors see patients virtually in remote areas. Pill bottles that know if medicine was taken. At Intel, we enable the technologies that are making healthcare, transportation, energy, retail and education even better. Because sponsoring tomorrow starts today.

intel.com/inside

Sponsors of Tomorrow.

Advertising Agency: MHC STUDIO   **Creative Director:** William Taylor   **Senior Designer:** Jason Scuderi

Illustrator: Simon Page   **Writers:** Kris Longwell, Karen McIntyre   **Client:** McGraw-Hill Construction

ASSIGNMENT

Prior to a tradeshow focusing on sustainability in architecture, where McGraw-Hill Construction was showcasing various and somewhat disconnected brands—GreenSource, Engineering News Record, Architectural Record, Dodge Construction Data, and Sweets Building Products—we were asked to develop a single ad that tied all the brands together in a simple way that the audience would appreciate.

APPROACH

Each of McGraw-Hill Construction's brands is a leader in its respective field. What the brands have in common, other than all being involved in the building industry, is that they perform vital roles across the spectrum of the Sustainability industry. We broke down the needs of the Sustainable profession into four essential elements and explained how the brands of McGraw-Hill Construction filled all of the essential needs of the Sustainability professional.

RESULTS

As this was a branding ad, results are hard to pinpoint; however, the show was a huge success. Our booth was the best attended booth of the show, our salesforce generated multiple leads, and our apps received over 200 downloads despite poor Internet reception.

WHAT IS ESSENTIAL?

KNOWLEDGE: The most extensive coverage of green-building trends, technologies, services, and innovations.

ACCESS: Comprehensive access to deep green product specifications, project data, and professional service providers.

VISIBILITY: Unprecedented exposure for your projects to the full range of green building and design professionals.

INSPIRATION: Derived from successful and exemplary leadership in conveying green building design and construction information.

Find it with McGraw-Hill Construction.

ARCHITECTURAL RECORD
DODGE
GREENSOURCE
SNAP
SWEETS
ENR

McGraw_Hill
CONSTRUCTION

Advertising Agency: Pennebaker   **Art Director:** Thomas Moczygemba   **Creative Director:** Jeffrey McKay

Writer: Debbie Mohr   **Client:** CDI Seals

ASSIGNMENT

The purpose of the Tuff Breed ads is twofold. First, being a new name in the industry, we wanted to build awareness for the product and brand name. Second, we wanted the ads to establish Tuff Breed as one of the top-performing well service packing products.

APPROACH

Our strategy involved giving the ad a personality and a voice that reinforced the image of a tough product made for tough conditions. We accomplished this by using big graphics featuring bold statements, such as "Bring it on," "No place for rookies," "A very bad day," and "Can eat your lunch."

Advertising Agency: Communica, Inc. **Art Director:** Jeff Kimble **Designers:** Ben Morales, Sonya Ives

Copywriters: Pat Pencheff, Susan Doktor **Account Director:** Barry Rosen, The Pursuit Group

Client: Severstal North America

ASSIGNMENT

Communica was asked by Severstal North America to develop a brand repositioning campaign to launch with a series of image and application trade ads.

The trade advertising was used to introduce the new brand positioning in the marketplace. The campaign was designed to set the stage for what would become a major consolidation and capital improvement initiative for Severstal.

Audiences include engineers, designers, purchasers, specifiers, and CEOs in the automotive, building, appliance, and agricultural manufacturing industries, as well as service center/distributors.

APPROACH

The new brand platform we created for Severstal positioned the company as a leader in the manufacturing of lighter, stronger, more flexible steel for a new manufacturing mandate requiring critical new application criteria. Just as importantly, the new positioning underlined Severstal's ability to move forward with more advanced product without sacrificing its customized, customer-centric service philosophy. In short, a company accelerating an industry-wide movement "one customer at a time."

The imagery and language provided a metaphor for this acceleration via individual customer collaboration and attention. Using steel as the visual common denominator in all of our image ads, we were able to telegraphically and uniquely communicate the brand value (Newton's Cradle, Dominos, Gears). Severstal steel becomes an agent for forward movement/progress. Severstal steel sets in motion a progressive acceleration of energy and momentum. The main visual is used against a blue background in order to elevate the image above the realm of everyday practicality and position it as larger than life/archetypal.

The simple, elegant design mirrors the clean, advanced manufacturing processes and the sophistication of Severstal technologies, processes, and equipment.

RESULTS

The campaign was enthusiastically received by both our North American and Russian-based clients. Excitement about the initial creative led to its adoption as a foundation for a comprehensive multi-channel digital and print program that has successfully differentiated the brand in a crowded marketplace.

MAKING STEEL SIMPLE.
ONE CUSTOMER AT A TIME.

We'll spell it out for you.
Severstal makes it easy for pipe and tube manufacturers to do business more efficiently and more profitably. Our newly modernized facilities produce both hot rolled and cold rolled products in the industry's widest range of widths and gauges. And we're strategically located to facilitate delivery of precisely the product you need at precisely the time you need it. That means lower transportation costs, decreased demand on your warehousing resources, tighter inventory management and better cash flow for you.

To learn more about Severstal North America visit www.severstalna.com or call 800-532-8857.

ACCELERATING
STEEL PERFORMANCE.

ONE CUSTOMER AT A TIME.

Severstal is driven. We're outdistancing the competition, and advancing steel technologies, products and processes. We're positioning our customers for success by investing in a new era of expanded capabilities. And we're focusing on our industry-leading facilities and renewing our commitment to unparalleled customer service and support.

To learn more about Severstal North America visit www.severstalna.com or call 800-532-8857.

Advertising Agency: rhed   **Creative Directors:** Del Terrelonge, Rico Bella, Jaime Vega   **Client:** rhed

rHed

(god gave noah the rainbow sign, no more water, the fire next time)

rHed

(all perceptions are borne with a single truth)

rHed

Advertising Agency: Struck, Inc.   **Executive Creative Director:** Steve Driggs   **Account Director:** Jeremy Chase

Art Directors: Nathan Wigglesworth, Dave Bunnell   **Account Manager:** Kelly McClelland

Copywriter: Garrett Martin   **Technical Creative Directors:** Abe Day, Joe Williamsen   **Client:** Utah Office of Tourism

Media Buyer: LOVE Communications

ASSIGNMENT

Create awareness of Utah as a premier vacation destination in a new market of busy commuters and city dwellers.

APPROACH

Working with media partner LOVE Communications, we pinpointed a golden opportunity at the Montgomery Street BART Station. With some coaxing, we convinced Montgomery Street to reach beyond their typical placement by printing on the walls, ceiling, and even the floor to create a forced-perspective where San Franciscans feel like they're standing at the base of Delicate Arch in Arches National Park. Once commuters pick their jaws up off the vinyl-wrapped floor, they're invited to share the view with a #visitutah hashtag and to start planning their escape to the majesty of Utah.

RESULTS

Full results of this Summer's Tourism is unknown, but web traffic to the UOT website increased 176% during this campaign, in addition to thousands of interactions across their social platforms.

Advertising Agency: Proof Advertising   **Art Director:** Craig Mikes   **Creative Director:** Dave Henke

Writers: Dave Pernell, Randall Kenworthy   **Client:** Baylor University

ASSIGNMENT

To raise awareness of Baylor's impact across the globe to proud alumni, prospective students, and parents.

APPROACH

We interviewed students and teachers about numerous Baylor student and mission trips all over the world to highlight. We then distilled the story down to a brief outcome statement that shows Baylor's global impact.

RESULTS

Admissions, applications, and interest continue to rise.

Show up late to this class and you might miss something huge.

Several hundred feet below the cows and pastures around Geneva, Switzerland sits the largest science experiment in the world. And among the renowned physicists and researchers selected to run it are students and professors from Baylor University. To them, testing theories on the formation of the universe by smashing protons together at a million times the heat of the sun is just another day of research. Research that could give students the experience of a lifetime. And yield the biggest scientific discovery of all time.

LARGE HADRON COLLIDER • CERN, SWITZERLAND

To learn more about Baylor's impact on the world, visit **baylor.edu/impact.**

BAYLOR ABOVE. BEYOND.

When communications failed, they tried a new language.

Surrounded by two of Earth's largest countries sits the tiny nation of Nepal. Within its borders, fewer than 40% of people speak the same language and far fewer can read it. So when Baylor music student Robert Moore had the opportunity to assist a divided country, he seized it. Moore spent 10 weeks in Kathmandu establishing the Nepal Music Educators' Society and writing a curriculum for Nepali schools. A curriculum that's helping the people of Nepal bond through the language that unites us all. Music.

NEPAL MUSIC EDUCATORS' SOCIETY • KATHMANDU, NEPAL

To learn more about Baylor's impact on the world, visit **baylor.edu/impact.**

BAYLOR ABOVE. BEYOND.

Advertising Agency: 160over90   **Executive Creative Director:** Jim Walls   **Creative Director:** Dan Shepelavy

Designer: Mike Burton   **Copywriter:** Brendan Quinn   **Client:** Nike Tennis

ASSIGNMENT

Develop creative concepts that promote the Nike Tennis 2011 Spring product line to the 14- through 17-year-old tennis player. Concepts must be flexible enough to work within a variety of channels (such as, retail stores, outdoor advertising, print advertising, online, etc.) across the globe, while leveraging Nike's top tennis athletes.

APPROACH

Before concepting, writing, or designing anything, we looked into Wimbledon's history, personality, and the culture surrounding the event. The idea was to pay homage to the proper customs and traditions, but do so in an irreverent attitude that would connect the brand with the 16-year-old competitive athlete. We accomplished this through aggressive typefaces inspired by punk rock, design elements such as the off-kilter crown and transparent yellow X, and carefully crafted headlines that offered punch and insight into both the game and the event.

Advertising Agency: BBDO Proximity MINNEAPOLIS   **Art Director:** Jason Craig   **Client:** HORMEL BLACK LABEL BACON

Creative Director: Derek Pletch   **Executive Creative Director:** Brian Kroening   **Copywriter:** Dave Alm

ASSIGNMENT

Americans have a fanatical love affair with bacon. We created a multi-city event called "The Bacon Throwdown," where bacon lovers could come together as a community to meet, eat, and compete in an all-out, no-holds-barred bacon-recipe contest. We created these fun and attention-grabbing posters to drive people to the event in each city.

APPROACH

While bacon lovers are serious about bacon, they have a sense of humor about that passion. We wanted our Bacon Takedown posters to be fun, colorful, and dynamic odes to pro boxing and wrestling posters of the past and present.

RESULTS

All the Bacon Takedowns held throughout the U.S. were sold out, and the success of the takedown events has led to the launch of a new Bacon Film Festival, where bacon maniacs can create and post their own bacon-inspired films.

THE NATIONAL BACON PARTY INVITES YOU TO

BACON TAKEDOWN
2·0·1·2

IT'S A NIGHT OF
WINNING
BELTS AND
LOOSENING
THEM.

20 BACON RECIPES
COMPETING
HEAD 2 HEAD

FOR YOUR FAVORITE
Vote
BACONTESTANT.

SUNDAY **MARCH 11**ᵀᴴ 2:00 until 4:00

SHANGRI-LA 1016 EAST 6ᵀᴴ ST. AUSTIN ★ TX

Hormel
Life Better Served

Find us and like us on
facebook.
facebook.com/HormelBacon

ADMISSION: $10
WWW.CHILITAKEDOWN.COM

Advertising Agency: Michael Schwab Studio | **Designer:** Michael Schwab | **Client:** James Whitburn, America's Cup 2013

ASSIGNMENT

Michael Schwab Studio was commissioned to commemorate the 2013 America's Cup sailing event on San Francisco Bay.

APPROACH

I wanted to create a graphic image that evoked the beauty, power, and drama of this historic event. My strategy was to avoid technical nautical design details and run with a "less is more" approach—typical of my graphic style.

RESULTS

The client was very happy with the results. I received several positive and intriguing comments such as: "Looks like sharks in the water," "The tilted water/horizon line really feels like the viewer is in motion," "The Golden Gate Bridge is a mythical presence watching over the race."

AMERICA'S CUP

SAN FRANCISCO 2013

AMERICA'S
CUP

Advertising Agency: Proof Advertising

Art Director: Rob Story

Creative Director: Craig Mikes

Writers: Rob Story, Scott Staab, Craig Mikes, Randall Kenworthy

Client: Moontower Comedy Festival

ASSIGNMENT

The assignment was to create ads and posters as part of a campaign launching the first-ever Moontower Comedy Festival. The intent was to create awareness of the festival and set the stage of the level of humor to expect.

APPROACH

We developed not only the name, logo, and website, but also traffic-generating ads and posters to drive interest to the site for ticket sales, even though some of the comedy acts were still being solidified. We didn't want to try to "out funny" the comics; instead, we opted to say that there are things said and done in comedy that you can't get away with in any other aspect of life, and then alluded to our festival as that place.

RESULTS

We heralded an initial year of success, including selling out the initial pre-sale passes. The Onion claimed the ads were the most viewed, and, as a bonus, posters were requested by acts Seth Meyers and Steven Wright.

BUSINESS MEETING

INAPPROPRIATE

MASTURBATION SKIT

THERE'S AN
APPROPRIATE
PLACE FOR INAPPROPRIATE
Humor

PARAMOUNT THEATRE PRESENTS
MOONTOWER
COMEDY AND ODDITY FEST
APRIL 25 - 28, 2012

12: VENUES 4: DAYS OVER 60: PERFORMERS

AUSTIN, TEXAS

MOONTOWERCOMEDYFESTIVAL.COM

133868

9301000121272

0.00 SEC: ORCH:R

ROW: F SEAT: 1

Advertising Agency: Butler, Shine, Stern & Partners   **Art Director:** Carrie Ammermann   **Client:** Sorel

Executive Creative Director: Mike Shine   **Associate Creative Directors:** Kelly Niland, Carrie Ammermann

ASSIGNMENT

SOREL was stuck. A victim of its own success, SOREL hadn't changed since 1962. The Caribou boots you bought in 1962 were the same ones you could be wearing today. And chances are, with SOREL's extreme durability, they'd still be functioning just fine.

APPROACH

SOREL had an honest, unpretentious, uncomplicated spirit that would allow us to play up its high-fashion credibility without sacrificing its utility. In 2009 and 2010, we set out to move SOREL from its original position as a tool for the snow to the emotional platform of stylishly utilitarian. This meant moving off the mountain and into the city, out of the snow and into fashionistas' hearts. From this mission, the campaign idea of Naturally Urban was born.

RESULTS

Results based on our objectives:

Drive SOREL sales to historic levels: Total global sales have increased from $45M in 2008 to $150M in 2011. Also inspired by the brand restage, SOREL gained over 200 new retail accounts in the U.S. in 2009, and sales at Nordstrom have increased from $86K in 2008 to $6M in 2011.

Build awareness of SOREL as a brand that blends function and fashion: The number of women who have heard of SOREL has increased significantly, from 31% to 38% between 2010 and 2011, with communication awareness increasing from 8% to 11% during the same period.

Increase brand trial and ownership: Nearly half (47%, up from 37%) of the women interviewed indicated either owning a pair of SOREL boots (24%) or at least trying them on (23%).

sorel.com

Après anything.   **SOREL**

Advertising Agency: LLOYD&CO	Creative Directors: Doug Lloyd, Jason Evans	Client: Oscar de la Renta

ASSIGNMENT

We aimed to create a dynamic, multifaceted campaign that captures the playful, optimistic spirit of the Spring/Summer 2012 collection.

APPROACH

We were inspired by the bright hues, billowing skirts, and luxurious dresses that walked down the Spring/Summer runway. The campaign is an organic extension of the collection's youthful, spontaneous energy.

RESULTS

There has been an overall excitement and buzz about the campaign, and the captivating new energy surrounding the brand.

Advertising Agency: LLOYD&CO   **Creative Directors:** Doug Lloyd, Conor Hautaniemi   **Client:** Bottega Veneta

ASSIGNMENT

The first goal was to find an artist who could capture the spirit of the S/S 12 Collection, both in the color palette and the lightness of the materials. Our second goal was to follow Bottega Veneta's long-standing tradition of working with artists in a collaborative way.

APPROACH

It is important for us to engage the Bottega Veneta client on a cultural level and not simply present a trend-directed message.

RESULTS

Both the client and professionals within the industry responded positively to the images and were impressed with the caliber of artist who worked with us on this fashion campaign.

BOTTEGA VENETA

Advertising Agency: SAGA.CG.SA   **Creative Director:** Christophe Gilbert   **Client:** KESHETT

ASSIGNMENT

We were approached by a jewel retailer in Australia that specializes in art deco jewels.

APPROACH

As the jewels are art deco, or similar in style, we researched the art made by artists during this particular period of time, ending up with a photographic-modern version of an art deco painting by Lempicka.

RESULTS

The jeweler came to Brussels to see the test we made and was astonished by the results. Unfortunately, once they had the test and went back to Australia, they never followed up on this project.

Keshett, when difference defines you.

KESHETT

Contemporary & Antique Jewellery

323 - 325 Little Collins Street, Melbourne, Victoria 3000   Tel: +61 3 9654 1514   Email: sales@keshett.com.au   Website: www.keshett.com.au

Keshett, when difference defines you.

KESHETT

Contemporary & Antique Jewellery

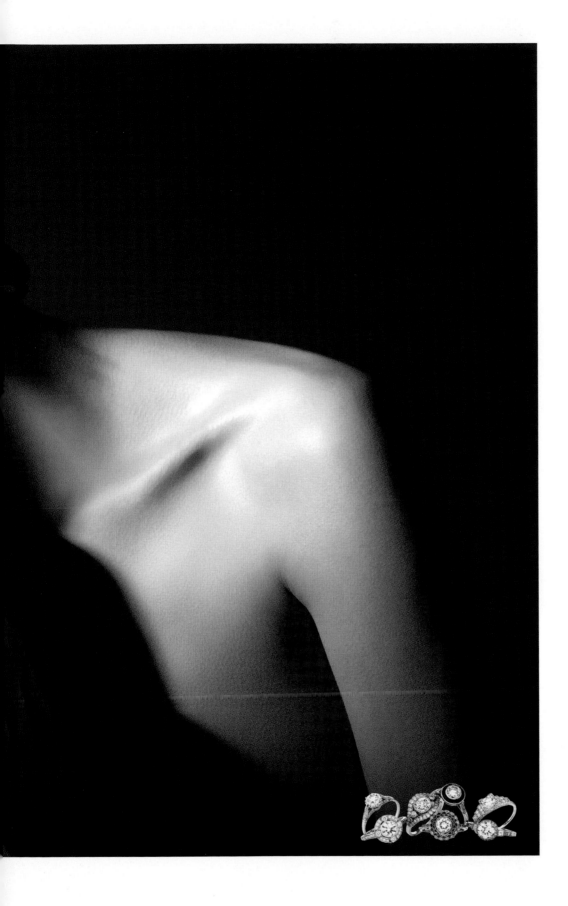

323 - 325 Little Collins Street, Melbourne, Victoria 3000   Tel: +61 3 9654 1514   Email: sales@keshett.com.au   Website: www.keshett.com.au

Advertising Agency: omdr design agency   **Art Director/Creative Director:** Osamu Misawa   **Photographer:** niwa

Designer: Mamoru Takeuchi   **Client:** WORLD Co., Ltd.

ASSIGNMENT

We were asked to create magazine advertising for COCOSHNIK, a fine jewelry brand. The advertising delivers COCOSHNIK's brand identity and their thought.

APPROACH

We developed new looks for the photography to best communicate the brand concept to readers.

Advertising Agency: Butler, Shine, Stern & Partners   **Art Director:** Gabrielle Tigan   **Client:** Piperlime

Executive Creative Director: Mike Shine   **Associate Creative Director:** Claudia Bruno   **Copywriter:** Lucas Zehner

ASSIGNMENT

For Piperlime's Spring 2012 campaign, the goal was to establish Piperlime as a destination for the fashion-forward—a place where she (and he) could find the best items from the brands she loves. The design and styling communicate the brand's fresh perspective on fashion and its lighthearted nature.

APPROACH

We wanted a design concept that showcased the product and presented Piperlime's point-of-view on the Spring trends, and demonstrated that while the brand loves fashion, it also believes that fashion needn't come with a capital F.

RESULTS

Not only was the campaign embraced internally, but it also delivered. During the campaign period, the brand saw a significant increase in traffic to the site, and several items featured in the ad quickly sold out.

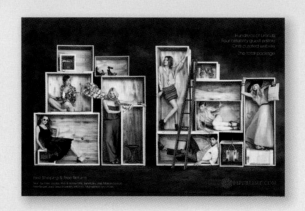

Hundreds of brands.
Four celebrity guest editors.
One curated website.
The total package.

Free Shipping & Free Returns
Marc by Marc Jacobs, Sam Edelman, Joie, Ray-Ban and more.

 PIPERLIME.COM

Advertising Agency: LLOYD&CO	**Creative Directors:** Doug Lloyd, Jason Evans	**Client:** Adidas Y-3

ASSIGNMENT

We aimed to create a campaign that embodies the vibrant duality of the Y-3 Spring/Summer 2012 pieces.

APPROACH

The Y-3 Spring/Summer 2012 campaign takes its cue from the experimental city of Brasilia. Portraits are collaged with xeroxes of archival Brasilia, to suggest a delicate balance between the body and the many ways it is contained.

RESULTS

The client was very pleased with the campaign, as the final images embodied the narrative we set out to relay.

Advertising Agency: Woodbine Agency　　　**Creative Director:** Vickie Canada　　　**Client:** Fruit of the Loom

Photographer: Kiyoshi TOGASHI

ASSIGNMENT

The goal of this three-piece Fruit of the Loom campaign was to illustrate the fine quality, textural detail, and rich color of the product and to play off the use of the word "fruit" in the company name and tie it into the photographs. They conceived of the idea to portray the insides of the fruits as being the actual Fruit of the Loom cotton.

APPROACH

To portray the insides of fruits as made of cotton, TOGASHI had to marry his graphic, still life photographs of the fruits with his photographs of the T-shirts. To achieve this goal, the T-shirt photographs were silk-screened with photographs of the actual insides of fruits. He had to carefully reconstruct and match the lighting and angle of the T-shirt shots with that of the still life shots and then merge them in post-production.

RESULTS

The result speaks for itself. The client and agency were thrilled with TOGASHI's pro-active, creative problem solving approach and the attention to every detail, which achieved three visually dynamic, elegant, and unique photographs.

fresh COLORS

Our new Heavy Cotton HD™ Collection offers a selection of colors that are fresher than ever.
With up to 29 stylish shades available, ranging in size from Youth XS through Adult 4XL, our color
offering is the perfect complement to your creativity. Now, having more of what you need means
choosing from a rainbow of looks that offer something for everyone. And the collection boasts one
of our densest fabrics yet, along with the same level of consistency and superior decorating
surface you expect from the always fresh, ever-colorful Fruit of the Loom® Activewear.

FruitActivewear.com | 888.378.4829

Advertising Agency: The Gate Worldwide   **Art Director:** Tim Ryan   **Client:** State Street Global Advisors

Creative Director and Writer: David Bernstein

ASSIGNMENT

This is a brand campaign for a precise family of investments called SPDR Exchange Traded Funds. The ads had to play off the tagline: "Precise in a world that isn't."

APPROACH

In these ads, we visualized the frustration of not being precise in everyday life. And then, in body copy, we explained how investing works the same way.

RESULTS

The ads tested better than any previous year, so the client was very happy with the results.

INVESTMENTS ARE LIKE ANNIVERSARIES.
YOU CAN'T BE A DAY LATE.

Truth be told, your spouse may forgive a

little tardiness. But the market won't. Ever.

So you may want to consider State Street's

family of SPDR® ETFs. They let you buy

and sell entire market segments just like

a stock. Which means you're always liquid.

Mid Caps. Commodities. Fixed Income.

No matter what you're interested in, we're

sure to have an investment that precisely

matches your investment strategy.

For details, visit spdrs.com and see if we

can improve your on-time performance.

SPDR
STATE STREET GLOBAL ADVISORS

Precise in a world that isn't.

IF YOU CAN'T BEAT THE MARKET, JOIN IT.

The market has a mind of its own. Trying to

predict which way it's headed is sometimes

an act of utter futility.

When the market moves, it doesn't send

out an engraved invitation. It just moves.

If you don't want to be left behind, State

Street has a suggestion: the SPDR S&P

500 Exchange Traded Fund.

Because it's an ETF, you can buy and sell

it as precisely as a stock.

With over 89 billion dollars in assets,

investors seem to think it's a big deal. If

you'd like to join the crowd, visit us at

spdrs.com for all the details.

SPDR
STATE STREET GLOBAL ADVISORS

Precise in a world that isn't.

Advertising Agency: WAX   **Art Director:** Hans Thiessen   **Creative Director:** Joe Hospodarec

Design Director: Monique Gamache   **Client:** Calgary Farmers' Market

ASSIGNMENT

Our goal was to let people know that the Calgary Farmers' Market is open all winter and has plenty of fresh and delicious food available—some of which happens to be especially cute.

APPROACH

We capitalized on the inherent cuteness of farm animals (a.k.a., free-range meat products). Then we synergized said cuteness with colorful—and equally cute—knitted balaclavas.

RESULTS

The fresh food consumers of Calgary felt warm and fuzzy all over—their wallets included.

Advertising Agency: Butler, Shine, Stern & Partners

Art Director: Nike Kamei

Executive Creative Director: Mike Shine

Associate Creative Directors: Shahin Edalati, Josh Leutz

Copywriter: Bem Jimmerson

Client: Mission Foods

ASSIGNMENT

Mission was the leader in the overall tortilla category, but was losing market share in the growing segment of "Better For You" products, which appealed to a health-minded, food-interested consumer. So, in August 2011, Mission launched a new line of premium tortillas made from unique, authentic, and healthy ingredients. Our task was to introduce Mission Artisan Style tortillas, spur trial and, ultimately, regain market share from the competition.

Mission had a delicious product. We needed to develop a campaign that would entice consumers seeking out new and interesting food experiences and get them to try Artisan.

APPROACH

There is a growing shift in food values in America. From over 7,000 farmers' markets and handcrafted beermakers to $6 cupcakes, gourmet food trucks, and celebrity chefs, food was becoming more than just nourishment. It's entertainment, it's a status symbol, and where it comes from matters. We wanted to show that Artisan had a place among these premium products.

We focused on a core segment dubbed Healthy, Wealthy, and Wise. They love to cook and take pride in sharing their efforts with family and friends. They see the ingredients in their pantry as a form of self-expression and are always on the lookout for new and unique foods and flavors. In addition, they look for quality ingredients and nutritional benefits.

To win over this target, we focused on the premium and unique ingredients in Artisan tortillas.

The campaign catches the tortilla up to the rest of the food world. Lettuce has gone from iceberg to arugula and frisee, meats are now free-range and grass-fed, and tequila is 100% agave. And now, Mission Artisan Style raises the bar for tortillas. With flax seed and blue corn, ancient grains, corn and whole wheat, and multigrain, Mission Artisan tortillas are not only worthy of the healthy stuff you put in them, they elevate your other ingredients to a whole new level. This is the tortilla for people who believe a microwave ding is not a dinner bell. It is *the* Top-Shelf Tortilla.

We knew that if people tried Artisan, they'd be hooked. So, we wrapped a giant food truck in Mission Artisan branding and sent it to food festivals in key markets to pass out samples, showcasing the product at its best. In addition, we supported the launch in out of home, food magazines, in-store POP, recipe cards, and online. We also were a featured product in an e-mail from Tasting Table, a free website/daily e-mail featuring the best in food and drink culture.

RESULTS

Our first few events served 6,000 to 8,000 samples each day, well above our expectations. And within 48 hours of launching our online campaign, over 50,000 coupons had been downloaded. The product sold well in key markets, gaining back market share from the biggest premium tortilla competitor. Mission is continuing to evolve the Artisan line with new flavors.

FOR THOSE
WHO BELIEVE THAT A
MICROWAVE DING
IS NOT A DINNER BELL.

Our handcrafted tortillas combine unique flavors, healthy ingredients and, of course, authentic taste.

The top-shelf tortilla

Advertising Agency: WAX   **Executive Creative Director:** Joe Hospodarec   **Art Director:** Brad Connell

Copywriter: Shannon King   **Illustrator:** Katherine Streeter   **Client:** Calgary Farmers' Market

ASSIGNMENT

Let people know that the Calgary Farmers' Market is open all summer and has plenty of fresh and delicious food available.

APPROACH

Continuing from the success of our winter campaign, which featured animals wearing toques and ski masks, we continued with the whimsical animal theme and featured pigs enjoying some summer fun and delicious food from the Calgary Farmers' Market.

RESULTS

Numbers are still pending, but it has been a very busy summer for the Calgary Farmers' Market. The client was thrilled with the final product and has requested an extension to the campaign through fall.

FRESH ALL SUMMER

Advertising Agency: WAX   **Art Director:** Brad Connell   **Copywriter:** Shannon King

Executive Creative Director: Joe Hospodarec   **Illustrator:** Katherine Streeter   **Client:** WURST

ASSIGNMENT

Our goal was to invite people to WURST—a new German-inspired beer hall and restaurant in Calgary—for Valentine's Day.

APPROACH

Subtlety—yeah, that sounds about right.

RESULTS

The ad went "almost-viral" on Facebook with over 700 Likes, helping make Valentine's Day at WURST the least subtle in town.

𝕳𝖆𝖕𝖕𝖞 𝖁𝖆𝖑𝖊𝖓𝖙𝖎𝖓𝖊'𝖘 𝕯𝖆𝖞

2437 4TH STREET SW · WURST.CA

WURST

Advertising Agency: Saatchi & Saatchi, New York

Copywriter: Aaron Alamo

Client: Novartis Lamisil

Creative Director: Joseph Pompeo

Art Director: Elena Dulin

ASSIGNMENT

Cracking dry feet is one of the most commonly misunderstood athlete's foot symptoms. To help clear up this issue, both in the consumers' minds as well as their feet, we wanted to create simple, yet standout executions to call attention to a pervasive issue where consumers are most bothered by their symptoms.

APPROACH

We created posters and ambient foot stickers for placement in high traffic areas—a provocative way to look at the issue of athlete's foot. We wanted to stop consumers literally in their tracks, so—to catch their attention in an unexpected way—we placed the stickers over the cracks in city sidewalks. The posters were placed in these areas so to interrupt people on their daily commute. Lamisil now has more top of foot awareness, and has gained a stronger foothold in the Athlete's Foot category as the best cure around.

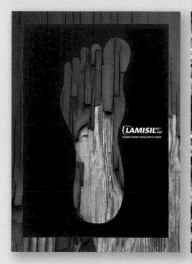

Advertising Agency: DeVito/Verdi   **Copywriters:** Wayne Winfield, Eric Schutte   **Client:** North Shore-LIJ Health System

Creative Director: Sal DeVito   **Art Director:** Manny Santos

ASSIGNMENT

Lenox Hill hospital has been a New York medical institution since the mid 1850s. A lengthy list of medical firsts, a patient base that includes the rich and famous, and a high-profile physician group have all been part of its rich history. The reputation and awareness of the hospital has diminished in recent years, due in large part to competitive efforts from larger hospitals that are Lenox Hill's neighbors. In an effort to help revitalize the hospital, our task was to generate heightened awareness of Lenox Hill as a significant New York institution.

APPROACH

With a goal of putting Lenox Hill back on the map, we leveraged the history of the hospital to create a New York voice with impact. Double-page spreads, spots with celebrity patients, and the use of other New York landmarks as visuals were used in print and TV ads.

RESULTS

In a pre/post study, the rating of Lenox Hill as the first place people think of for quality medical care increased by almost nine percentage points after the first year of the campaign.

WE HAD CARDIOLOGISTS BEFORE THE CITY HAD ARTERIES.

The New York of 1857 was a far cry from the New York of 2011. For that matter, it was a far cry from the New York of 1911. The word *In the 1850s, heart care was something mysterious practiced by very few doctors.* "infrastructure" had yet to be coined – which was only fitting, since there was virtually none to speak of. Sanitation was a disgrace and transportation wasn't much better. People traveled on foot or via horse-drawn carriages. There were few major roads and no major arteries.

But at Lenox Hill Hospital, doctors were already making major inroads of their own. Here, at what was then called the German Hospital and Dispensary, these early medical pioneers were busy developing innovative treatments for a wide range of heart and vascular diseases, like inflammation of the heart, insufficient aortic valve and narrowing of the mitral valve.

These doctors helped establish Lenox Hill Hospital's reputation in the area of cardiology before it was even known as cardiology – a reputation it continued to maintain and enhance for the next 150 years.

Early members of our medical staff. Without many of the benefits of modern medicine, these physicians made critical strides in the rapidly developing field of cardiology. Today, our reputation for excellence can be traced directly to them.

In 1967, Lenox Hill Hospital opened the first cardiac care unit in the metropolitan area. In the 1980s, Dr. Gary Roubin co-invented the Gianturco-Roubin Flex Stent, the first coronary artery stent approved by the FDA, and became the first to transplant it into a patient. In 1994, Dr. Valavanur Subramanian originated minimally invasive coronary bypass surgery, and continues to play a vital role on our cardiac team along with Dr. Roubin. No wonder other doctors come to Lenox Hill Hospital to learn about advanced procedures like radial artery intervention, transeptal catheterization, carotid stenting and more.

But Lenox Hill Hospital is renowned for much more than just cardiac services. Our Department of Orthopedic Surgery is recognized by health experts throughout the nation for its pioneering treatments of a broad range of musculoskeletal conditions, with a special emphasis on the development of minimally invasive procedures.

In 1884, publisher Oswald Ottendorfer helped fund a new East Village location.

Lenox Hill Hospital is also home to the Nicholas Institute of Sports Medicine and Athletic Trauma (NISMAT). Founded in 1973 by Dr. James Nicholas, it was the first hospital-based center in America dedicated to the study of sports medicine.

The Department of Otolaryngology – Head and Neck Surgery is recognized as one of the busiest centers in the Greater New York area for thyroid and parathyroid gland surgery, facial plastic and reconstructive surgery, and more.

Built in 1857, the German Hospital and Dispensary moved in 1905 to its present location at East 77th Street.

At The Center for Maternal-Fetal Medicine, our internationally renowned perinatologists provide high risk newborns with a complete range of advanced obstetric care and services.

Few realized it at the time, but Lenox Hill Hospital's powerful legacy was already growing amidst the chaos of 19th century New York.

Lenox Hill Hospital has one of the largest full-service robotics centers in the Northeast. From cardiac bypass and prostate cancer treatments to head and neck surgery and gynecologic oncology procedures, robotic technology provides minimally invasive surgical solutions to complex medical problems improving patient outcomes.

And now that Lenox Hill Hospital has joined forces with North Shore-LIJ, it's easier than ever to see why, 154 years after opening its doors, it remains New York's hospital of choice. And thanks to significant improvements in the city's infrastructure, getting there has become a whole lot easier.

MODERN MEDICINE BEFORE MEDICINE BECAME MODERN.

1857. According to the date, it was the second half of the 19th century. But as far as medicine was concerned, it was the middle ages. In fact, if the truth be told, the word medicine was something of a misnomer. Because for all intents and purposes, it owed less to science than superstition. Doctors operated totally in the dark: They could hardly be expected to know the cures for diseases when they didn't know the causes.

But in New York City, the makings of a major medical milestone were underway. It began with the first stone laid on a construction site on Park Avenue and 77th Street. It culminated in the completion of an imposing new facility that would ultimately become known as Lenox Hill Hospital.

The quality of care was unprecedented, which is what one would expect considering the quality of the staff. The doctors were true pioneers who set about providing a cure for the primitive practices of the day.

The doctors on the Lenox Hill Hospital staff were pioneers who contributed to some of the greatest medical breakthroughs of their time.

Dr. Henry Jacques Garrigues introduced antiseptic obstetrics to North America. Dr. Willy Meyer performed some of the country's earliest pulmonary surgery. Dr. Abraham Jacobi was considered the father of American pediatrics, while Dr. Carl Eggers and Dr. Dewitt Stetten were founding members of the American College of Surgeons.

The procedures they developed and implemented ultimately became the essential components of modern medicine.

Lenox Hill Hospital's list of firsts is impressive to say the least (although given the staff, that's not surprising).

Both laymen and doctors could see a big difference between Lenox Hill Hospital and other hospitals.

Among them are the first general hospital in New York City to open a tuberculosis division. The country's first physical therapy department. One of the first intensive care units in New York City. And the first

One of New York City's first hospitals, but more importantly, one of medicine's pioneering facilities.

1897 – One of the first X-ray machines in the U.S. • 1938 – The first angiocardiography performed in the country.

1967 – The first cardiac unit in New York City. • 1973 – The first hospital based center in the nation for the study of sports medicine.

2009 – New York's first totally endoscopic robotic coronary artery bypass surgery.

angiocardiogram in the United States was performed by William H. Stewart, a former director of Radiology. The first successful esophagectomy for carcinoma, performed by Dr. Franz Torek. And the first coronary angioplasty performed in the U.S., by Dr. Simon Sterzer.

For 154 years, Lenox Hill Hospital has served New Yorkers right from the heart of Manhattan.

The list never stopped growing. Neither did Lenox Hill Hospital's stature, as it continued to break new ground in two new centuries.

Not that Lenox Hill Hospital plans to rest on its laurels. It has joined forces with North Shore–LIJ, a testament to its ongoing commitment to provide the best clinical treatment in

Lenox Hill Hospital, formerly known as the German Hospital and Dispensary, as it looked in 1868.

New York. Indeed, investments in Lenox Hill Hospital will build on the hospital's well-deserved reputation for excellence in all areas, including cardiac care, digestive disorders and orthopedics.

The fact is, Lenox Hill Hospital has been at the forefront of innovation for the past 150 years. It's an enviable position to be sure. One that Lenox Hill Hospital has no intention of relinquishing.

Advertising Agency: STIR   **Executive Creative Director:** Bill Kresse   **Digital Artist:** Brian Steenstry

Associate Creative Director and Writer: Scott Shalles   **Photographer:** Jeff Salzer   **Client:** St. Joseph's/Candler

ASSIGNMENT

The assignment for the agency was to inform potential patients about the advanced technology, procedures, and compassion found at St. Joseph's/Candler.

APPROACH

Healthcare advertising tends to all look the same. This execution stands out by allowing the doctor to tell a story about a specific patient and procedure. The art direction complements the story with a variety of sincere and engaging images.

RESULTS

The inspirational nature of this execution resonated well with the consumer, which put a smile on our client's face.

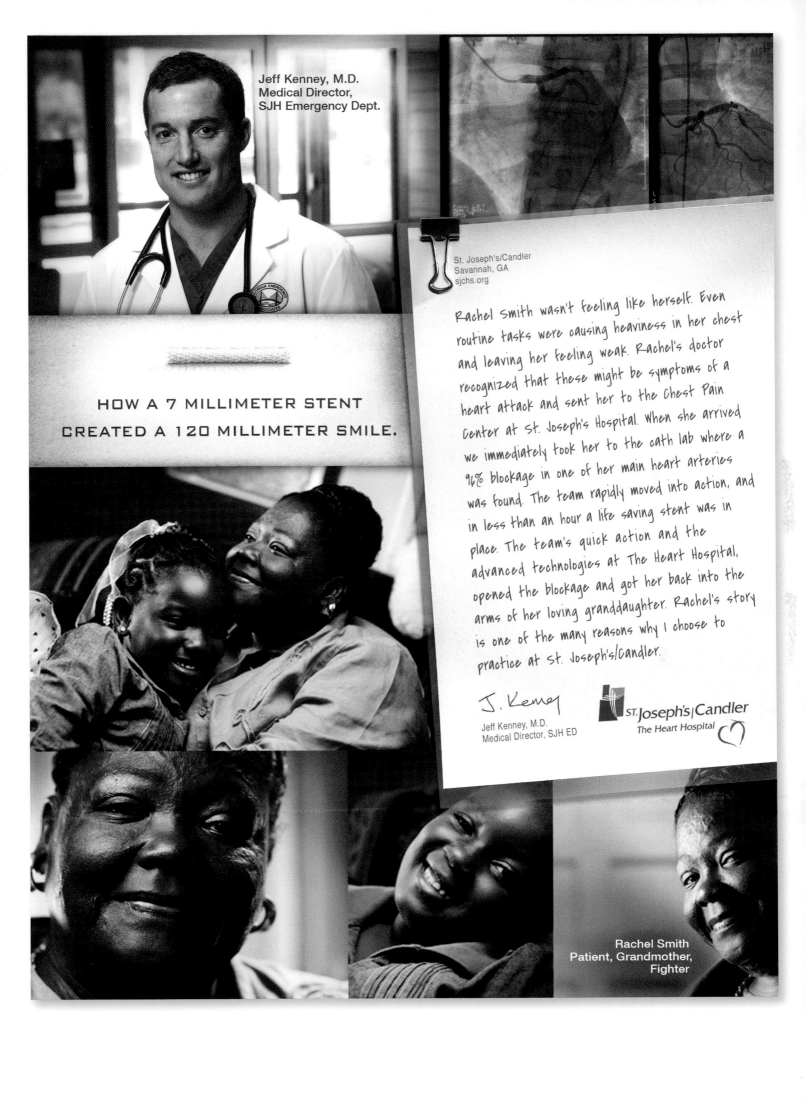

Jeff Kenney, M.D.
Medical Director,
SJH Emergency Dept.

HOW A 7 MILLIMETER STENT
CREATED A 120 MILLIMETER SMILE.

St. Joseph's/Candler
Savannah, GA
sjchs.org

Rachel Smith wasn't feeling like herself. Even routine tasks were causing heaviness in her chest and leaving her feeling weak. Rachel's doctor recognized that these might be symptoms of a heart attack and sent her to the Chest Pain Center at St. Joseph's Hospital. When she arrived we immediately took her to the cath lab where a 96% blockage in one of her main heart arteries was found. The team rapidly moved into action, and in less than an hour a life saving stent was in place. The team's quick action and the advanced technologies at The Heart Hospital, opened the blockage and got her back into the arms of her loving granddaughter. Rachel's story is one of the many reasons why I choose to practice at St. Joseph's/Candler.

J. Kenney

Jeff Kenney, M.D.
Medical Director, SJH ED

ST. Joseph's | Candler
The Heart Hospital

Rachel Smith
Patient, Grandmother,
Fighter

Advertising Agency: BVK

Creative Director: Rich Kohnke

Writer: Mike Holicek

Retoucher: Jim McDonald

Photographer: Nick Collura

Producer: Allison Lockwood

Client: The Children's Hospital at OU Medicine

ASSIGNMENT

The Children's Hospital wanted to communicate that it is uniquely prepared to help kids deal with the fear and stress of visiting the hospital. The ads were intended to create awareness of the hospital's dedicated children's specialists and to drive parents to a landing page where they could share with their kids an interactive experience that would show them what to expect when they come to the hospital.

APPROACH

We wanted to symbolically portray the kind of anxiety and fear a child might feel visiting a hospital for the first time. We chose typical rooms within the hospital to insert imaginary creatures that represent "scary" in a simple, arresting way. By showing various hospital personnel physically removing the creatures, we quickly made it clear that everyone at The Children's Hospital is here to help "remove" the fear.

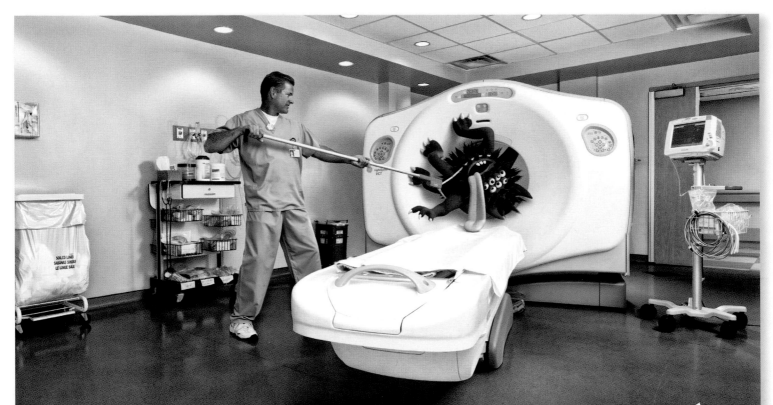

KIDS HAVE FEARS. **WE REMOVE THEM.** The **Children's** Hospital at OU Medical Center

You'd be surprised what a child can imagine a hospital to be. So treating kids starts with helping them understand medical terms, and helping prepare them for what to expect. At The Children's Hospital we're experts at taking away the anxiety. We specialize in the unique needs of children, using equipment and techniques designed just for them. And our research puts us at the forefront of the smartest new ideas and innovations for keeping kids healthy. Show your child what to expect at **GoodbyeFears.com.**

KIDS HAVE FEARS. **WE REMOVE THEM.** The **Children's** Hospital at OU Medical Center

Kids can imagine the worst when it comes to a hospital visit. That's why The Children's Hospital has Child Life specialists, trained to show them that what they think is often scarier than what's real. So they can feel safer during their stay. Here an experienced team of doctors, nurses and staff are trained in pediatric medicine, using equipment and procedures designed specifically for children. And our drive to bring the latest advances means even greater peace of mind. Show your child what to expect at **GoodbyeFears.com.**

Advertising Agency: Bailey Lauerman　　**Art Director:** Ron Sack　**Writers:** Nick Main, Marty Amsler　　**Designer:** Brandon Oltman

Creative Director: Carter Weitz　　　　**Finish Art:** Joe Liebentritt　　**Digital Retouch:** Gayle Adams

Account Executive: Michellle Sukup　　　**Client:** The Negro Leagues Baseball Museum

Photography: National Baseball Hall of Fame Library, Cooperstown, NY

ASSIGNMENT

Challenge: Increase awareness and support for the Negro Leagues Baseball Museum (NLBM) by driving attendance and donations through a branding campaign.

Context: With new leadership in place for the museum, as well as an increasing need for donations due to the lackluster economy in recent years, the client challenged us to help them become a respected institution to which individuals and corporations can feel confident donating.

Audience: Baseball fans, history fans—people who are wired into the sport. They may have been to Cooperstown and DC, but NLBM is a new dimension for them to explore their passions. For the Kansas City community, we wanted to emphasize that the NLBM as an important part of the city.

APPROACH

A series of posters was developed to promote the Negro Leagues Baseball Museum in Kansas City, Missouri. Singing the praises of these unsung heroes, these messages turned the spotlight on the courageous athletes who played not for fame or money, but because they loved the game. Prints were made and donated to the museum for sale in the gift store and for general promotion.

Design rationale: Images of the teams were placed in the lower portions of the poster, away from the other elements, in order for the viewer to get an idea of the isolation these players felt.

RESULTS

On top of the impressive sales at the museum itself, the posters have been featured in *Communication Arts* March 2012 edition.

Discover Greatness.

On June 21, 1925, the all-black Wichita Monrovians faced off against the Wichita Ku Klux Klan baseball club. And for nine innings, the baseball field became a level playing field. Although no pictures remain from the actual game, the Monrovians won, 10 to 8. Stories that provoke. Stories that inspire. They're all waiting for you at The Negro Leagues Baseball Museum. Visit. And take home a story of your own. **nlbm.com**

AFTER YEARS OF TERROR AND INTIMIDATION, THEY FOUND A WAY TO HIT BACK.

Photo courtesy of the National Baseball Hall of Fame Library, Cooperstown, NY.

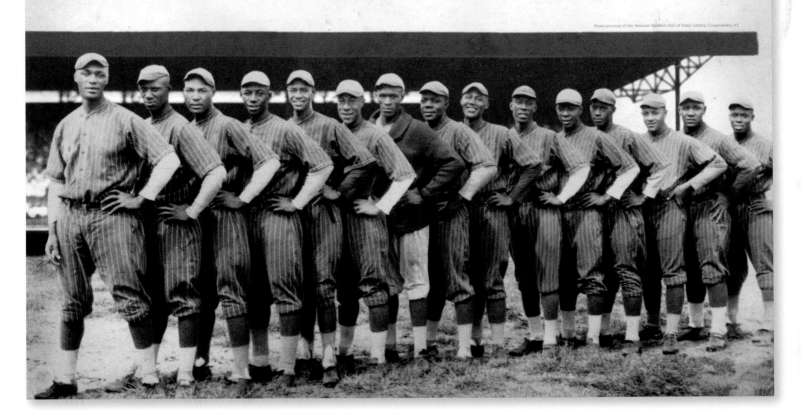

Advertising Agency: Peter Mayer Advertising   **Creative Director:** Tony Norman   **Copywriter:** Mike Heid

Art Director: Richard Landry   **Client:** WWII Museum

ASSIGNMENT

The agency was tasked to promote the opening of the The National WWII Museum.

APPROACH

Our approach was to give it a little New Orleans flare, because that is where the World War II Museum is located.

IN NEW ORLEANS, THE BATTLE OF THE BULGE HAS NOTHING TO DO WITH FOOD.

While New Orleans is best known for its Creole cuisine, it's also home to The National WWII Museum. Come stand on the front lines of history, and experience war in the first person. Don't miss *Beyond All Boundaries*, the 4D experience showing exclusively at the Solomon Victory Theater.

Open 7 days a week, 9am - 5pm
Andrew Higgins Dr. between Camp and Magazine Streets
504.528.1944 | www.nationalww2museum.org

Advertising Agency: STUDIO INTERNATIONAL   **Creative Director:** Boris Ljubicic   **Client:** Clavis - Music Teachers Association

ASSIGNMENT

Motif: How to play Chopin—a poster made for the 200th year anniversary of that great piano virtuoso.

APPROACH

The poster was made for Clavis - Music Teachers Association. It is an international piano school in which professional teachers exchange experiences and teach piano playing. The designer presented their unusual way of teaching—by playing on interior blinds—and then visualized Chopin's sonates being played in the same manner. Moving fingers on blinds allows more or less light to pass, and that is rhythmically shown here in 100 images. Some images repeat, because some sequences in musical script are repeated.

RESULTS

The poster is exceptionally well received by school students and teachers, because it develops in their imagination sound "images"—similar to those a piano forms when under their fingertips. By the way, the windows in the school hall have exactly the same type of blinds, so that is humorously explored.

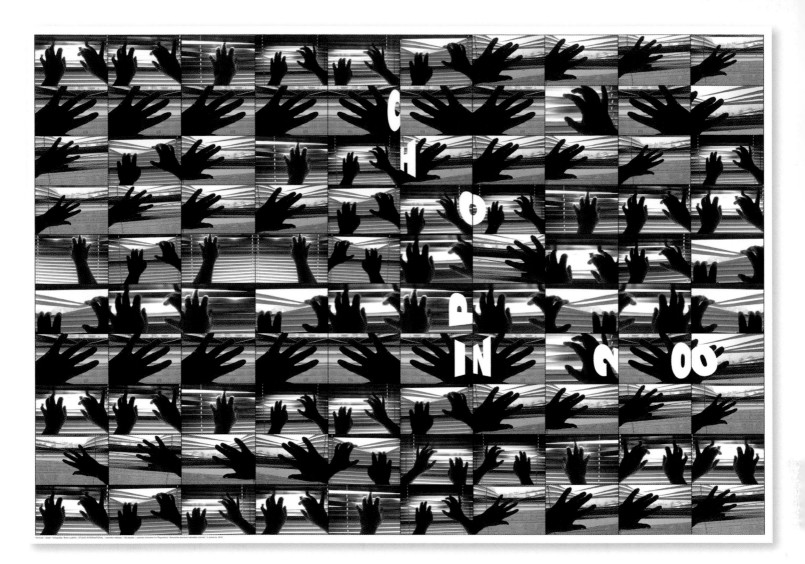

Naravost – dizajn · fotografija: Boris Lukšič· STUDIO INTERNATIONAL · izdelava nabodala· 126 disajev · v sklopu koncerta· Ca. Filgradija· Komunitka skanela hakladne Ljbniani 2 ptemea 2012

Advertising Agency: TBWA, Chiat, Day   **Global Director of TBWA\Worldwide:** Lee Clow   **Executive Creative Director:** Patrick O'Neill

Chief Creative Officer : Rob Schwartz   **Creative Directors:** Bob Rayburn, Patrick Condo

Associate Creative Directors: Becca Morton, Gage Clegg, Eric Haugen   **Senior Art Directors:** Brandy Cole, Kirk Williams

Senior Copywriter: Charlie Stephenson   **Senior Designers:** Jason Fryer, Bory Chung   **Client:** The Recording Academy

ASSIGNMENT

The Music is Life is Music poster campaign is one component of a larger platform designed to drive viewership to the 53rd annual GRAMMY Awards. The campaign is rooted in a simple insight: the music an artist creates is inspired by the life the artist lives. Each execution brings this insight to life by visualizing the defining events and places of a GRAMMY-nominated artist.

APPROACH

Through research and interviews, we identified the most defining moments of a GRAMMY artist's life. A celebrity list was developed, which included Lady Gaga, Eminem, Katy Perry, Ceelo Green, Arcade Fire, and Justin Bieber. We then concepted and developed visuals that represented those key moments. Exposing everything from stories of their humble beginnings, to breakout moments that ultimately led them to the GRAMMY stage.

RESULTS

The 53rd GRAMMY Awards was the most watched GRAMMY Awards show in ten years, attracting 26.7 million viewers.

MUSIC IS LIFE IS MUSIC

THE 53rd GRAMMYs
SUNDAY FEB 13 8PM ONLY CBS ●2HD
musicislifeismusic.com

MUSIC|IS|LIFE|IS|MUSIC

THE 53rd GRAMMYs
SUNDAY FEB 13 8PM ONLY CBS ◉2–
musicislifeismusic.com

MUSIC|IS|LIFE|IS|MUSIC

THE 53rd GRAMMYs
SUNDAY FEB 13 8PM ONLY CBS ◉2–
musicislifeismusic.com

MUSIC|IS|LIFE|IS|MUSIC

THE 53rd GRAMMYs
SUNDAY FEB 13 8PM ONLY CBS ◉2–
musicislifeismusic.com

MUSIC|IS|LIFE|IS|MUSIC

THE 53rd GRAMMYs
SUNDAY FEB 13 8PM ONLY CBS ◉2–
musicislifeismusic.com

MUSIC|IS|LIFE|IS|MUSIC

THE 53rd GRAMMYs
SUNDAY FEB 13 8PM ONLY CBS ◉2ᴴᴰ
musicislifeismusic.com

Advertising Agency: Syrup NYC   **Art Director:** Mike Meadus   **Creative Director:** Mike Meadus   **Client:** Bayer CropScience

ASSIGNMENT

To show how Bayer CropScience is dedicated to helping farmers meet the world's rising food demands through innovative farming technology.

APPROACH

The world is growing—and so, too, are the number of mouths to feed. Conversely, the amount of usable land for agriculture is decreasing. The substitution of forks for the wheat crop illustrates both the demand for food production and Bayer's commitment to helping farmers meet this growing need.

RESULTS

The ad generated a positive association with Bayer CropScience and increased goodwill for the organization. The publication received an estimated readership of 400,700.

Through relentless innovation, we help Canadian farmers feed a hungry planet.

Bayer CropScience

06/12 - BCS12042

Advertising Agency: Colle+McVoy   **Executive Creative Director :** Mike Caguin   **Group Creative Director:** Eric Husband

Creative Director: Brian Ritchie   **Art Director:** Derek Till   **Art Buyer:** Chris Peters

Retoucher: Greg Goranson   **Photographer:** Jonathan Chapman   **Client:** Nestle Purina

ASSIGNMENT

For those in the "fancy," dog shows are more than just a casual interest, they are a life-consuming passion. Their dogs are not pets, they're elite athletes that represent years of hard work and dedication. This work is a celebration of that commitment, heroically depicting their pride and joy as the center of their universe.

APPROACH

At one of the nation's top dog shows, we shot documentary-style photos of the candid moments between dogs and humans. Then, we created ads to inspire our target audience, from seasoned champion to first-time rookie, by addressing one of the universal truths that compels them all to compete—the shared belief that "This could be the year."

RESULTS

The dog show community embraced our ads, sharing them with social media. Purina® Pro Plan® remained the top dog food for the "fancy," and was fed to 90 of the top 100 show dog champions.

Advertising Agency: Leo Burnett Warsaw

Art Directors: Sylwia Rekawek, Justyna Nakielska

Creative Directors: Pawel Heinze, Krzysztof Iwinski

Client: Procter & Gamble

ASSIGNMENT

The goal was to create posters that would communicate that washing your clothes with Dreft protects their shape, and also that Dreft is a fashion-friendly product.

APPROACH

We show that if you are wearing clothes that lost their original shape, you are actually losing your own shape. We suggest that if you want to protect your shape, you should use Dreft washing liquid.

RESULTS

The clients loved it.

Advertising Agency: serviceplan   **Client:** A. W. Faber-Castell Vertrieb GmbH

Designers: Alexander Schill, Matthias Harbeck, Oliver Palmer, Andreas Balog, Nicolas Becker, Lorenz Langgartner, Marijo Sanje

ASSIGNMENT

The campaign shows, in an impressive and humorous way, the true-to-life colours of Faber-Castell crayons—in the truest sense of the word: True Colours.

APPROACH

In an unseen and impressive way, the colour fastness and diversity of Faber-Castell crayons is shown. The link between object and crayon shows how realistically you can colour, and positions Faber-Castell crayons as the best tool for the realization of creative ideas.

Advertising Agencies: Moth Branding and 14-forty   **Art Director:** Ben Nicolas   **Creative Director:** Pam Patterson

Designer: Dain Blodorn   **Copywriter:** Carrie Sedor   **Client:** Prudential Ltg.

ASSIGNMENT

Create an ad that introduces and inspires desirability for the Pulse—a new product designed to create a sense of movement within a rectilinear space—while also repositioning Prudential Ltg. as an innovator and forward-thinking architectural lighting design company.

APPROACH

After interviewing the California lighting designer, we gained a clear understanding of the design inspiration. The undulating nature of the fixture (as it is expressed in rows), pays homage to the Southern California coast and the rhythms of the waves. We selected the imagery to strategically position the product's design centric luminaire by emphasizing the sculptural form as referenced by the surfboard. The ad runs in trade publications that focus either on architecture or lighting design—the nature-based imagery stands out remarkably in this setting. The Where's Waldo effect and the headline—"inspire and de(light)"—serve to amplify these factors in execution.

RESULTS

The ad created great awareness for the launch of this dynamic fixture, generating six-figure orders within weeks of its introduction, and now it is a core addition to Prudential Ltg.'s linear family of fixtures. We were also honored to win an award for the ad's creativity from *Architectural Record* magazine, the preeminent trade publication in the industry. The awards banquet at their annual trade show served to further expose many lighting designers and architects to the ad and the Pulse lighting product's introduction.

inspire and de(light)

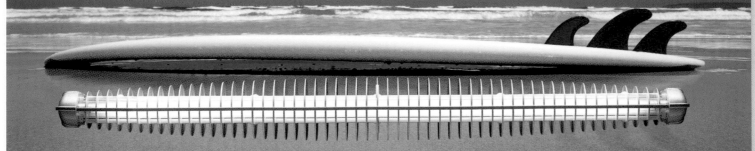

These are the emotions of innovation and change. Prudential's brand new, luminous homage to the cool design culture of the California coast and the rhythm of the ocean. Prudential shines with the new pulse of innovation. See the inspiration, Pulse fixture and facts online at **prulite.com/pulse**.

pulse

PRUDENTIAL LTG.

Advertising Agency: DDB Dubai, UAE   **Art Director:** Firas Medrows   **Creative Directors:** Shehzad Yunus, Firas Medrows

Client: Clorox Company

ASSIGNMENT

When left unprotected, or inappropriately protected, food loses its flavor—or worse. Food with milder flavors will take on dominant flavors from their surroundings.

APPROACH

We have stretched this thought of flavor migration and visually demonstrate the concept in a manner that will stop consumers in their tracks as the insight resonates with them. The surprise in the visuals only goes to show the need to segregate and store food correctly, using Glad products, in order to preserve taste and flavor integrity.

Advertising Agency: DDB Dubai, UAE   **Creative Directors:** Shehzad Yunus, Kartik Alyer, Makarand Patil

Art Director: Makarand Patil   **Client:** Clorox Company.

ASSIGNMENT

Establish the stain-removal ability of Clorox for Colors—an additive used while washing clothes.

APPROACH

The idea is a simple demonstration of how easy it is to remove stains with Clorox for Colors, represented by showing stains made out of interlocking plastic bricks.

RESULTS

The simplicity of the print campaign helped us extend the idea into an activation in prominent hypermarkets.

EASY-TO-REMOVE
Ink Stains

EASY-TO-REMOVE
Ketchup Stains

Advertising Agency: Havas Worldwide Bangkok Co., Ltd. **Art Director:** Krisda Chamchuen

Production Manager: Chainarong Watanathanakun **Photographer:** Remix/Nok

Account Executive: Koblarp Narukatpichai **Illustrator:** Anuchai Secharunputong **Creative Director:** Sitthaichai Okkararojkij

Copywriter: Sitthichai Okkararojkij **Director:** Asawin Phanichwatana **Client:** Shieldtox Naturgard

Advertising Agency: Havas Worldwide Bangkok Co., Ltd. **Art Director:** Krisda Chamchuen

Production Manager: Chainarong Watanathanakun **Photographer:** Remix/Nok

Account Executive: Koblarp Narukatpichai **Illustrator:** Anuchai Secharunputong **Creative Director:** Sitthaichai Okkararojkij

Copywriter: Sitthichai Okkararojkij **Director:** Asawin Phanichwatana **Client:** Shieldtox Naturgard

Natural Protection

Natural Protection

Advertising Agency: Syrup NYC   **Creative Directors:** Barbara Waibel, Uwe Schneider   **Art Director:** Kersten Knoedel

Photographer: Steffen Jahn   **Client:** d&b audiotechnik GmbH

ASSIGNMENT

d&b audiotechnik is a well-known manufacturer of excellent professional loudspeaker systems designed for live performances. For the very first time, they built extremely small loudspeakers—and this was the requested message: Very small professional reinforcement systems for live applications.

APPROACH

The ad campaign visualizes both sonic sound (curves) and live atmosphere (light). Titles with a wink and helical copy texts—like the visualized curves—tell about the teenyweeny size of these new loudspeakers.

RESULTS

The client is running the campaign in more than 180 special interest magazines around the world.

Teenyweeny nearfills. Live.

d&b audiotechnik

www.dbaudio.com

The E4 loudspeaker is just a little bit smaller than a pint of beer.
A coaxial built miniature, with a conically symmetric 100° directivity.
Made for even reinforcement in the near field, it can be mounted
in any orientation, and is almost invisible. While it sounds distinctively
bigger than it is, it remains neutral, clear, transparent and intelligible
even at high sound pressure levels. As with all the little systems
in the d&b E-Series.

d&b
audiotechnik

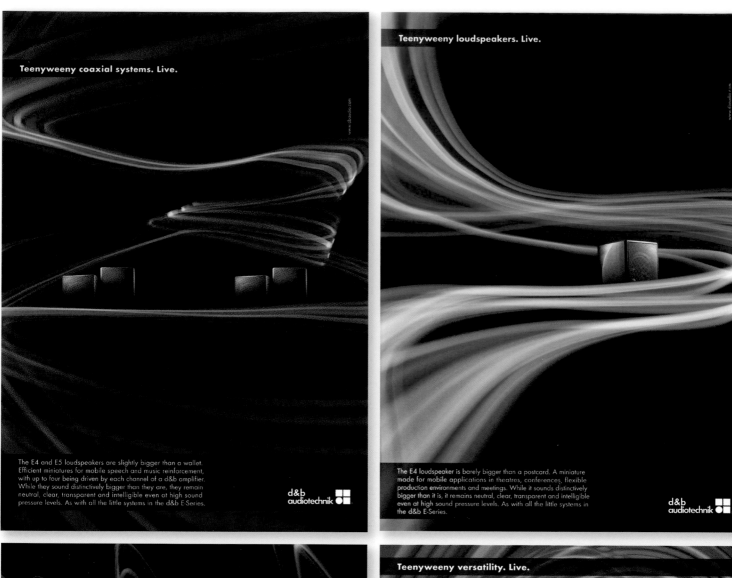

Teenyweeny coaxial systems. Live.

www.dbaudio.com

The E4 and E5 loudspeakers are slightly bigger than a wallet. Efficient miniatures for mobile speech and music reinforcement, with up to four being driven by each channel of a d&b amplifier. While they sound distinctively bigger than they are, they remain neutral, clear, transparent and intelligible even at high sound pressure levels. As with all the little systems in the d&b E-Series.

d&b
audiotechnik

Teenyweeny loudspeakers. Live.

www.dbaudio.com

The E4 loudspeaker is barely bigger than a postcard. A miniature made for mobile applications in theatres, conferences, flexible production environments and meetings. While it sounds distinctively bigger than it is, it remains neutral, clear, transparent and intelligible even at high sound pressure levels. As with all the little systems in the d&b E-Series.

d&b
audiotechnik

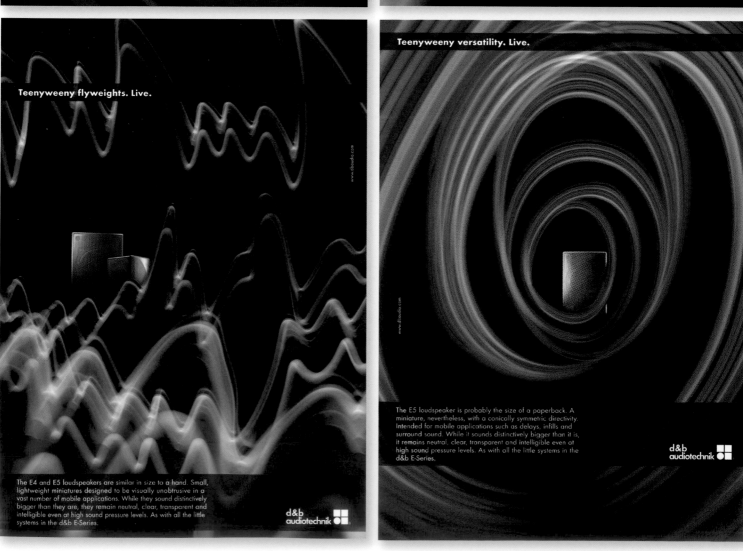

Teenyweeny flyweights. Live.

www.dbaudio.com

The E4 and E5 loudspeakers are similar in size to a hand. Small, lightweight miniatures designed to be visually unobtrusive in a vast number of mobile applications. While they sound distinctively bigger than they are, they remain neutral, clear, transparent and intelligible even at high sound pressure levels. As with all the little systems in the d&b E-Series.

d&b
audiotechnik

Teenyweeny versatility. Live.

www.dbaudio.com

The E5 loudspeaker is probably the size of a paperback. A miniature, nevertheless, with a conically symmetric directivity. Intended for mobile applications such as delays, infills and surround sound. While it sounds distinctively bigger than it is, it remains neutral, clear, transparent and intelligible even at high sound pressure levels. As with all the little systems in the d&b E-Series.

d&b
audiotechnik

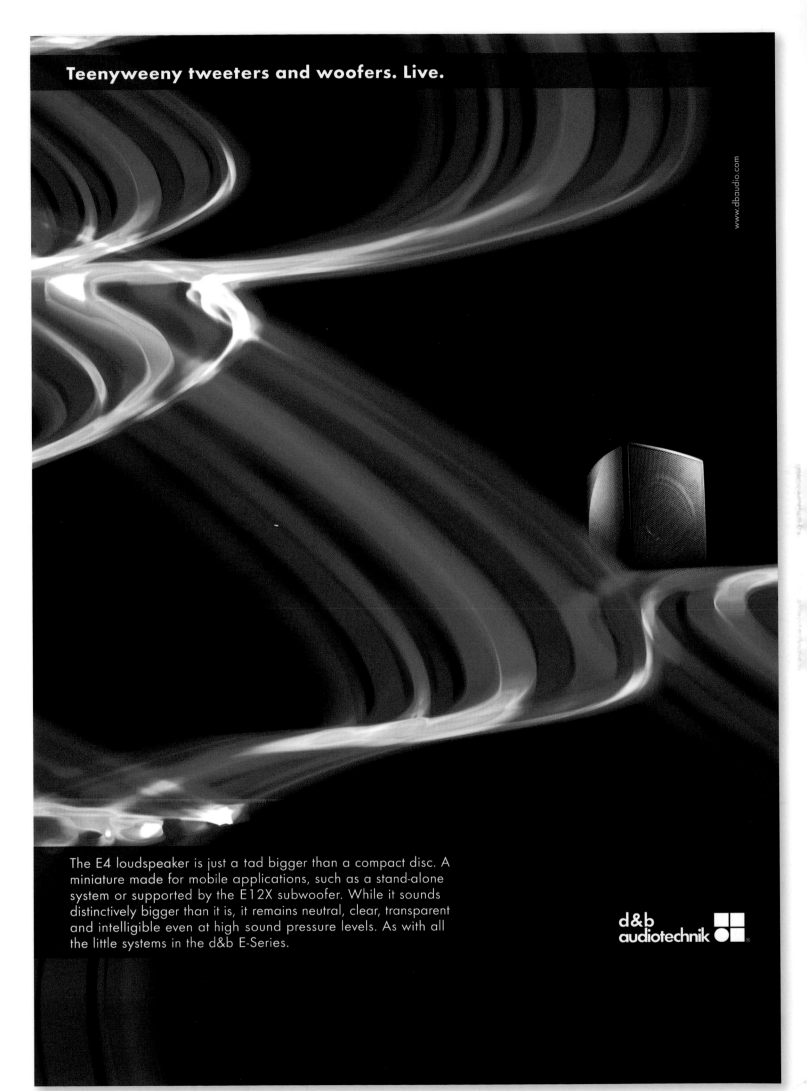

Advertising Agency: Bailey Lauerman   **Art Director:** Jim Buhrman Jr.   **Creative Director:** Carter Weitz

Photographer: Bob Ervin, The 42   **Copywriters:** Neveen Hegab, Cliff Watson   **Digital Retouch:** Joe McDermott

Project Manager: Alex Maltese   **Account Executive:** Derek Peterson   **Client:** Cargill

ASSIGNMENT

Communicate the benefits of Sweet Bran, a feed ingredient used in cattle finishing rations, to feed lot managers and nutritionists.

APPROACH

No one had really branded an ingredient like this before. In the past, communication consisted of facts and figures, not advertising and certainly not a brand. Our bold statements and branding attitude brought a very disruptive idea to this market.

SWEET BRAN

SUPER-SIZED
LONG BEFORE
THEY LAND
ON A BUN.

A Cargill Product

SWEET BRAN

A **Cargill** Product

TREATS CATTLE LIKE POODLES OWNED BY RICH OLD LADIES.

Advertising Agency: Syrup NYC   **Executive Creative Director:** Ted Tsandes   **Senior Art Director:** Jeremy Oviatt

Creative Directors: Jill Bustamante, Reid Thorpe   **Photographer:** Josh Wood

Senior Copywriter: Kara Hallstrom   **Client:** Dymo

ASSIGNMENT

We were tasked with introducing new LabelManager printers to businesses. With new features, such as a bigger LCD screen that displays label effects and a rechargeable ion battery, these printers would be an easy way for any business to shape up their organization.

APPROACH

Who says labels can't be fun? By combining the long continuous label strip from the DYMO LabelManager printers and the ancient Japanese art of Origami, we created ads that were both informative and entertaining. By using a long strip of label tape, we were able to create shapes, such as a file folder, rechargeable battery, and scissors. It's through these iconic shapes that we could highlight organizational issues in the office and show how the LabelManager printer could address them. And since these shapes are labels, it only made sense to display the headlines as if they were printed directly on them.

RESULTS

The campaign helped create differentiation with the product in a very generic retail space.

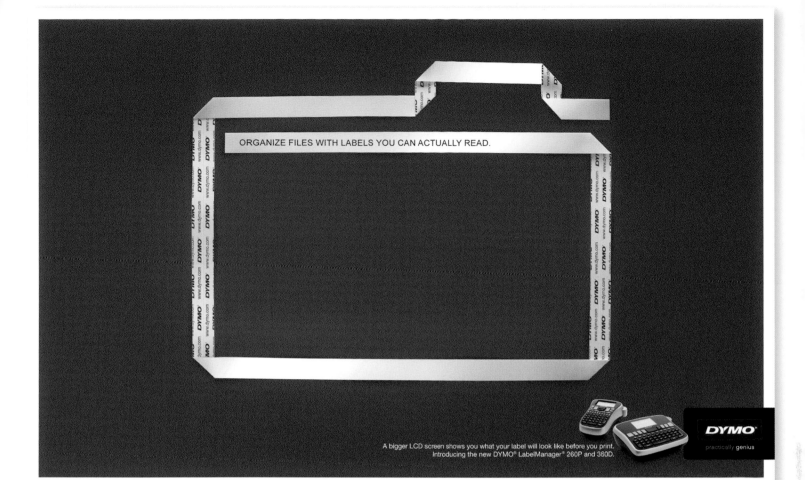

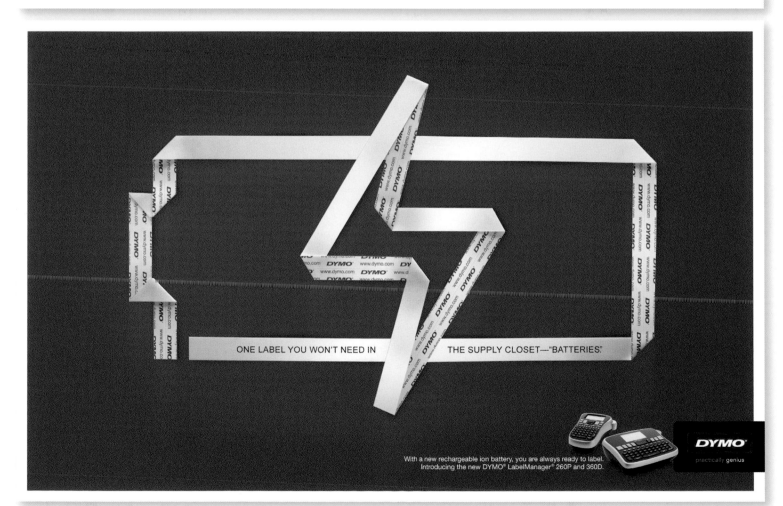

Advertising Agency: Bailey Lauerman   **Art Director:** Jim Buhrman Jr.   **Creative Director:** Carter Weitz

Copywriter: Neveen Hegab   **Digital Retouch:** Joe McDermott   **Project Manager:** Alex Maltese

Account Executive: Derek Peterson   **Client:** Cargill

ASSIGNMENT

Showcase the benefits of feeding RAMP, a starter ration for cattle.

APPROACH

RAMP's tagline, "Right to the bunk," creates a link between the brand and the primary interest of the feeder—to quickly get cattle on feed. By placing our product and cattle in the gutter, or "bunk," of the magazine spread, we created an effective piece of communication that was disruptive in the market.

RESULTS

RAMP has secured more than 25% market share after just the first eighteen months of availability.

Advertising Agency: Communica, Inc.

Account Director: David Kanaraowski

Designer: Ben Morales

Copywriter: Pat Pencheff

Client: BASF North America

ASSIGNMENT

BASF Polyurethanes, one of BASF North America's largest divisions, provides innovative solutions for a myriad of industries, ranging from automotive and packaging to building materials and textiles. It was critical that the advertising campaign reflect and reinforce the BASF brand platform. Target audiences included CEOs, designers, engineers, purchasers, and other channel influencers for a wide range of original equipment and tier manufacturers applications.

APPROACH

The BASF global brand positioning line is "We create chemistry." It is the articulation of their value platform—bringing added value and quality to everyday living by providing sustainable solutions for everyday living.

RESULTS

The unanimously enthusiastic response to this campaign has led to an upsurge of interest in BASF's variety of sustainable solutions. The campaign has also been warmly received by the client in Europe, where North American creative work is seldom used. Several of the ads were repurposed and included in prestigious international collateral and advertising.

Advertising Agency: pp+k

Executive Creative Director: Tom Kenney

Associate Creative Director: Michael Schillig

Copywriter: Michael Schillig

Art Director: Trushar Patel

Client: Gulfshore Bird-A-Way and Spider Control

ASSIGNMENT

Our assignment was to create a very bold and attention-getting poster for a small, relatively unknown company's spider control service. We wanted to first and foremost create more awareness for this company and ultimately generate more business.

APPROACH

We intentionally came up with a concept that couldn't help but get noticed and arouse someone's curiosity. Who wouldn't be drawn to a poster that encouraged people to hire a professional killer to get rid of someone they despised? We reasoned that if anyone had a spider problem, Gulfshore was the one company they would remember and hire to take care of the problem—quick and easy with no questions asked. We tried to make our visual image just as chilling as the headline, featuring a silhouetted figure in the doorway with a weapon that is actually a pest control sprayer.

RESULTS

Since the client's budget was very limited, we knew we had to do something that would get talked about. The poster's bold, tongue-in-cheek headline and chilling visual have definitely had a powerful impact on people. They've helped create awareness for the company and have led to more inquiries and business.

HIRE A PROFESSIONAL KILLER TO GET RID OF SOMEONE YOU DESPISE AT THE OFFICE

Our spider control and web removal service will do the job

Over the years, we've killed zillions. Well, spiders that is. So don't let some creepy critters take over your office, warehouse, or home. Put a contract out on them. Our spider control and web removal service will do the job clean and fast with no questions asked. Just call 813.661.4738 or visit us at gulfshore-birdaway.com

GULFSHORE BIRD-A-WAY AND SPIDER CONTROL

Advertising Agency: Doe Anderson   **Art Directors:** David Vawter, Scott Troutman, Scott Boswell   **Client:** Maker's Mark

ASSIGNMENT

The project was to create a holiday mailer to be sent to Maker's Mark's most loyal customers, our Ambassadors, to demonstrate how much we value their devotion to the brand, and do it in a way consistent with Maker's brand personality—friendly, approachable, not taking itself too seriously. In addition to showing our Ambassadors how much we value their loyalty, we wanted to encourage them to share their holiday gift and their love for the brand with friends.

APPROACH

The solution was to give their favorite bourbon something they never knew it needed: a tiny, tacky holiday sweater, perfectly tailored to a 750ml bottle of Maker's Mark. Of all the ideas we developed, we felt this was the one most likely to be shared by our Ambassadors with fellow Maker's drinkers and potential consumers.

RESULTS

By virtue of the thousands of Facebook postings and photos of bottles, pets, and babies wearing the sweater, we (and the client) deemed the program a success. The brand is currently on allocation (all available inventory sold through), and volume increased 19% in 2011. As the client was so pleased, it was decided to extend the idea into retail activation.

Advertising Agency: Goodby, Silverstein & Partners

Photographer: Claude Shade

Creative Director: Rich Silverstein

Client: Golden Gate National Parks Conservancy

ASSIGNMENT

On May 27, 2012, the Golden Gate Bridge celebrated its 75th anniversary. We were asked to create new and unique imagery that highlighted the beauty of the bridge and commemorated this historic event.

APPROACH

The Golden Gate Bridge is an icon and a cliche. I was trying to take one of the most photographed icons in the world and make people see it in a new way. My decision was to show angles and details that people haven't seen before. Our photographer was given unprecedented access to all parts of the bridge, with the objective of capturing images that pay tribute to the perfect symmetry between design and engineering. Stylistically, I was highly influenced by the Russian and German avant-garde movements.

GOLDEN GATE BRIDGE

75TH ANNIVERSARY

Advertising Agency: pp+k   **Executive Creative Director:** Tom Kenney   **Creative Director and Copywriter:** Joey Crawford

Senior Art Director: Javier Quintana   **Junior Art Directors:** Ariana Durkin, Palmer Holmes   **Client:** Serenity Mission

ASSIGNMENT

Serenity Mission helps those who suffer from the grip of addiction. Our assignment was to create an awareness that Serenity Mission puts people on a lifelong path of recovery by offering them a way to escape the disease that has taken over their life.

APPROACH

We created a series of print ads that clearly demonstrated how many people who suffer from addiction can feel trapped in that lifestyle. Through this campaign, we positioned Serenity Mission as the "way out" and as a beacon of hope in an otherwise dark world.

it's time we help you help you

serenitymission

We'll help you regain the life you lost to addiction and guide
you through this lifelong journey of recovery.

serenitymission.com

it's time we help you help you.

serenitymiss.com

We'll help you regain the life you lost to addiction and guide
you through this lifelong journey of recovery.

it's time we help you help you.

We'll help you regain the life you lost to addiction and guide
you through this lifelong journey of recovery.

serenitymission
LIVING WITH YOURSELF

serenitymission.com

Advertising Agency: pp+k   **Executive Creative Director:** Tom Kenney   **Associate Creative Director:** Michael Schillig

Copywriter: Michael Schillig   **Art Director:** Trushar Patel   **Client:** The Pediatric Cancer Foundation

ASSIGNMENT

Our assignment was to create a poster campaign that would tell the Pediatric Cancer Foundation's unique story in a very original, powerful, and emotional way. We wanted this to be very visually driven and immediately capture the attention of many consumers. Our goals were to really touch people and ultimately increase awareness and donations.

APPROACH

Through these posters, we wanted to portray a child's fight against cancer in a totally different way than normally seen. Instead of using typical dramatic images of children suffering with cancer, we decided to show what kids would really like to do to cancer—with a little help from their toys. And thanks to the Pediatric Cancer Foundation's nationwide collaboration of top doctors and researchers, they're trying to make these children's dreams come true as soon as possible by attacking cancer in new ways that will lead to a less toxic, more targeted cure.

RESULTS

The campaign has garnered lots of attention and has been very well received by the client and public. People like how it empowers children and symbolically communicates their courage to stand toe-to-toe with cancer and fight it. This ties in perfectly with the Pediatric Cancer Foundation's philosophy to bring together the nation's top doctors and researchers to ultimately find a cure. As the first-ever creative poster campaign produced for the Pediatric Cancer Foundation, these ads have raised more conversations at foundation events and created more awareness than ever before. In fact, the posters were so well liked that the Pediatric Cancer Foundation still has them hanging up at their corporate office.

PEDIATRIC CANCER
FOUNDATION
Funding Research. And Hope.
fastercure.org | (813) 269-0955

Kids with cancer imagine the day when they can turn the tables on this monstrous disease and actually attack it. That day is here as the Pediatric Cancer Foundation has formed a nationwide collaboration of top doctors and researchers, who are performing clinical trials to fast-track a cure. Together, with your support, we can help children stand up to cancer and beat it.

Advertising Agency: Dunn&Co. **Creative Director:** Troy Dunn **Associate Creative Directors:** Glen Hosking, Dan Stevenson

Art Director: Grant Gunderson **Photographer:** Dave Spataro **Client:** Florida Department of Transportation

ASSIGNMENT

Florida has the highest pedestrian death rate in the United States, and the fatality rate for bicyclists is more than double the national average. We were awarded the assignment to create an awareness campaign that would save Floridians from themselves.

APPROACH

Research showed that the average motorist, pedestrian, and bicyclist are blind to the basic rules of the road. So we created an awareness platform called See The Blindspots to encourage Floridians to open their eyes to the facts and see the roads differently. We then created a 360° campaign that portrayed vehicles as far more menacing objects than usual in order to motivate pedestrians, motorists, and bicyclists to be more cautious.

RESULTS

Our friends at the Florida Department of Transportation were awestruck by the quality of the work. They asked us to create something that wouldn't be ignored, but never expected a campaign that looked like this. Supported by print, television, outdoor, radio, and a controversial online video that received political attention, global news coverage, and over a quarter of a million views, SeeTheBlindspots.com received 119,000 visits in its first month. New data has not yet been collected, but the goal is to reduce fatalities by 20% before the year 2015.

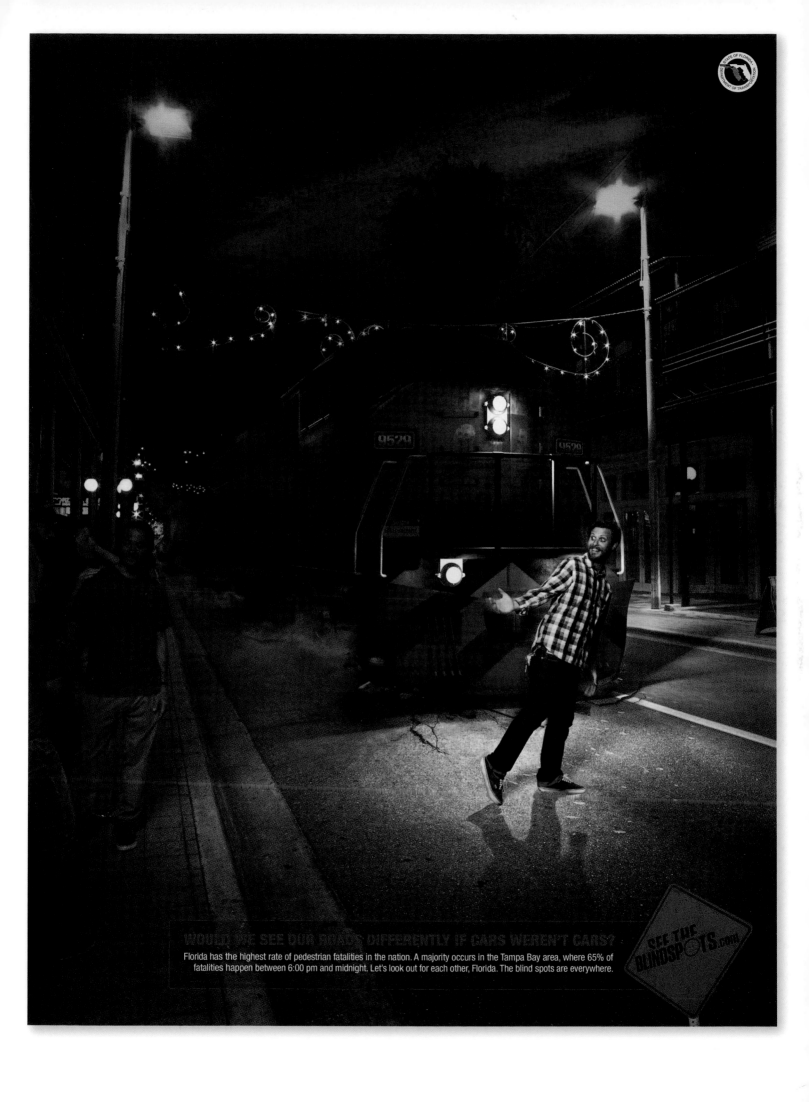

WOULD WE SEE OUR ROADS DIFFERENTLY IF CARS WEREN'T CARS?

Florida has the highest rate of pedestrian fatalities in the nation. A majority occurs in the Tampa Bay area, where 65% of fatalities happen between 6:00 pm and midnight. Let's look out for each other, Florida. The blind spots are everywhere.

SEE THE BLINDSPOTS.com

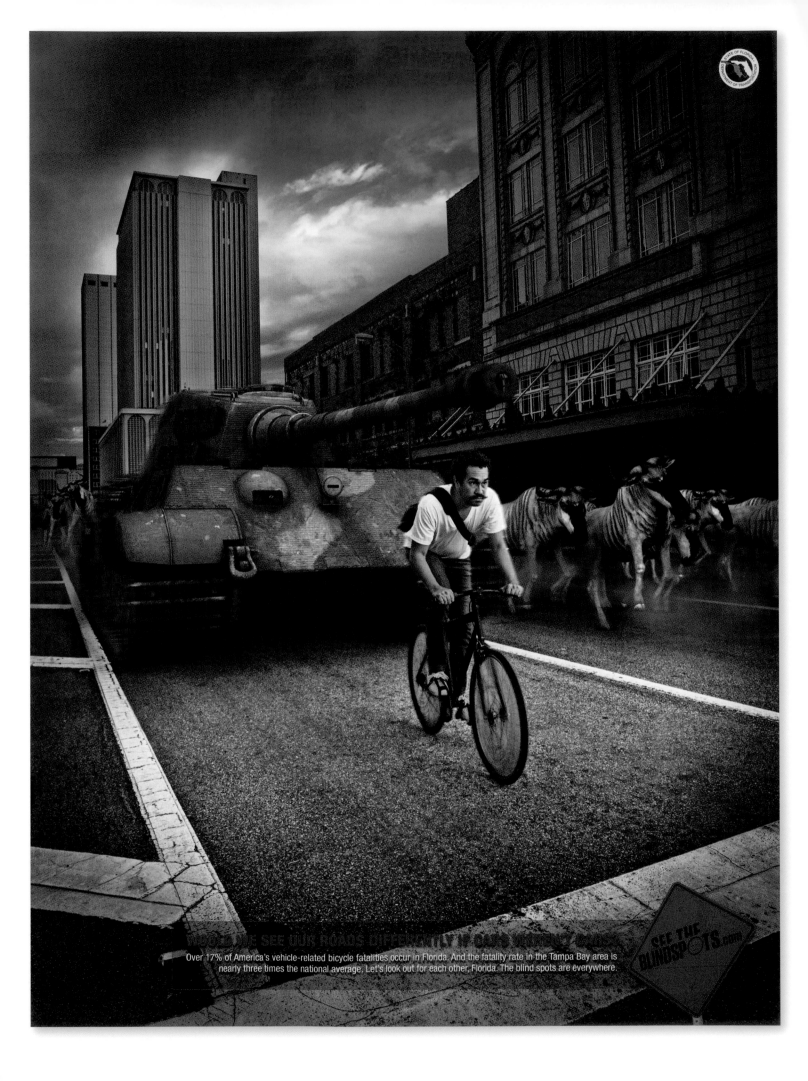

Nine pedestrians are killed in Florida every week. Many of these deaths are the result of pedestrians making dangerous judgments when crossing the street. Let's look out for each other, Florida. The blind spots are everywhere.

SEE THE BLINDSPOTS.com

Advertising Agency: IAL Saatchi & Saatchi Pakistan

Chief Creative Officer and Art Director: Ali Mumtaz

Strategy: Nida Haider, Assam Khalid

Creative Director: Shaheryar Ghayas

Writer: Jamil Akhtar

Photographer: Insiya Syed

Client: Depilex Smile Again Foundation

ASSIGNMENT

Depilex Smileagain Foundation's mission is to help female survivors and victims of acid burns in Pakistan by providing them appropriate medical attention and reconstructive surgery, psychological/psychiatric support, shelter, and vocational training. The project's goal was to create social awareness and sensitivity by working toward the complete eradication of this heinous crime.

APPROACH

Our approach was to create a moving piece of communication that would not only highlight the unpleasantness of an acid attack, but would also leave the viewer with a sense of hope for the victims.

RESULTS

The client was delighted with the response the communication received, not only in terms of spreading awareness, but also in support.

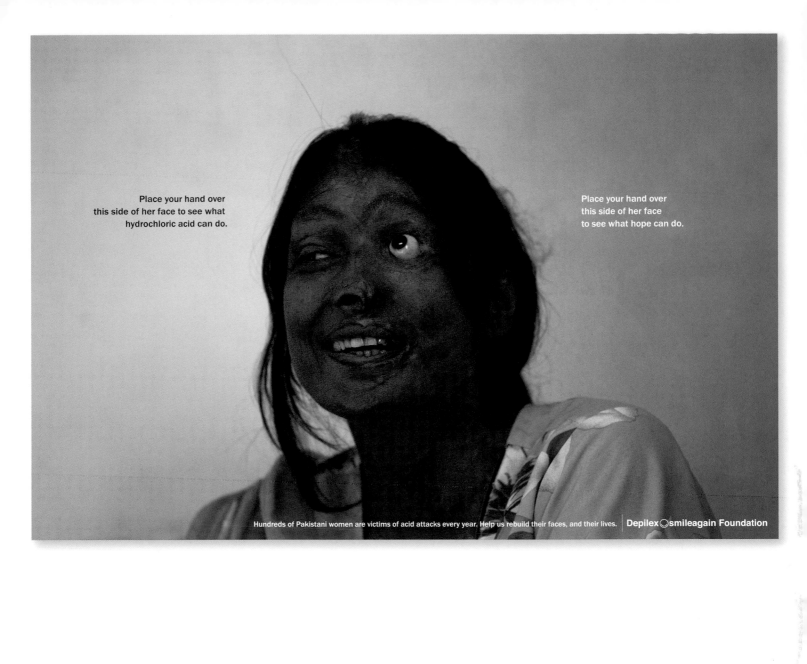

Place your hand over
this side of her face to see what
hydrochloric acid can do.

Place your hand over
this side of her face
to see what hope can do.

Hundreds of Pakistani women are victims of acid attacks every year. Help us rebuild their faces, and their lives. | Depilex ◯ smileagain Foundation

Advertising Agency: 14-forty   **Creative Director:** Pam Patterson   **Art Director:** Benjamin Nicolas

Designer: Dain Blodorn   **Copywriter:** Melanie Casparian   **Client:** I Am Waters

ASSIGNMENT

Create an ad that evokes intrigue, entices the reader to engage emotionally with the cause, informs readers of the current state of homelessness in America (e.g., families, children, veterans lack of access to clean drinking water), and demonstrates the aspirational words on the packaging—dream, hope, peace, and love. The call to action should drive readers to visit the website for additional information to better understand the complexities of the issue and how I Am Waters is committed to providing for the American homeless.

APPROACH

The cause is an unusual one that begs some explanation. We felt that to provide a layer of meaning atop the packaging, and thereby create a sort of puzzle, would engage the audience, as well as begin to intrigue, inspire, and inform. This is one in a series of four ads, each based upon a different word of the packaging. Each ad utilizes different demographics within the local homeless community—families, elderly, veterans, children, and the handicapped. The call to action is then delivered in the form of a question—do you know how many families are homeless in America today?—or the appropriate question for that demographic.

RESULTS

The ad raised awareness, the website saw a doubling of traffic over the media run, and the ad series culminated in a successful, sold-out fundraising event that served to raise over a half a million dollars.

HOW DO YOU DREAM WHEN YOU ARE HOMELESS?

Sharing a Dream™
iamwaters.com

I Am Waters provides fresh water and inspiration to the homeless. Do you know how many families are homeless in America today? Visit us online to discover the startling answer and learn more about how you can help. Share the dream at **iamwaters.com**

I AM WATERS
FOUNDATION
iamwaters.com

READ
Buy the book
and participate
in the dream.

WATCH
See videos of
homeless parents
and their children.

DONATE
No homeless person in
America should suffer
from lack of water.

Advertising Agency: Syrup NYC   **Art Director:** Rich Kohnke   **Creative Director:** Gary Mueller

Writer: Mike Holicek   **Client:** Milwaukee Health Department

ASSIGNMENT

The Milwaukee Health Department wanted to educate mothers about important steps to increase the odds of having a healthy baby. The outdoor and guerilla campaign needed to address a range of issues, including breast feeding, prenatal checkups, smoking cessation, and nutrition—all key factors that would contribute to lowering Milwaukee's unacceptably high infant mortality rate.

APPROACH

We decided to use playful exaggeration to demonstrate the benefits of promoting a stronger, healthier baby. A range of babies would be featured, performing obviously impossible feats of strength, to stop our target in her tracks and then deliver one key health message per execution.

RESULTS

The campaign has generated over 15 million earned media impressions in the past year. And 72% of inner city focus group respondents, when asked to recall a health-related advertising campaign they liked, answered "strong baby."

Eat Healthier
BEFORE HE'S BORN FOR A
STRONGER
baby AFTER.

CITY OF MILWAUKEE HEALTH DEPARTMENT
iwantastrongbaby.com

Advertising Agency: Wieden & Kennedy   **Creative Directors:** Ben Terrett, Michael Bow   **Client:** The Guardian

ASSIGNMENT

The aim was to publicize a daily series of articles in *The Guardian* newspaper, analyzing the causes of the riots in Britain in the Summer of 2011

APPROACH

"Broken Britain" was an expression much used over the period of the riots, so we chose to represent this literally. Photographer Jonathan Knowles was commissioned to create an image in which a glass map of Britain was shot with a gun, and captured before the pieces fell. The colors were introduced in the photography, and are from *The Guardian* brand palette.

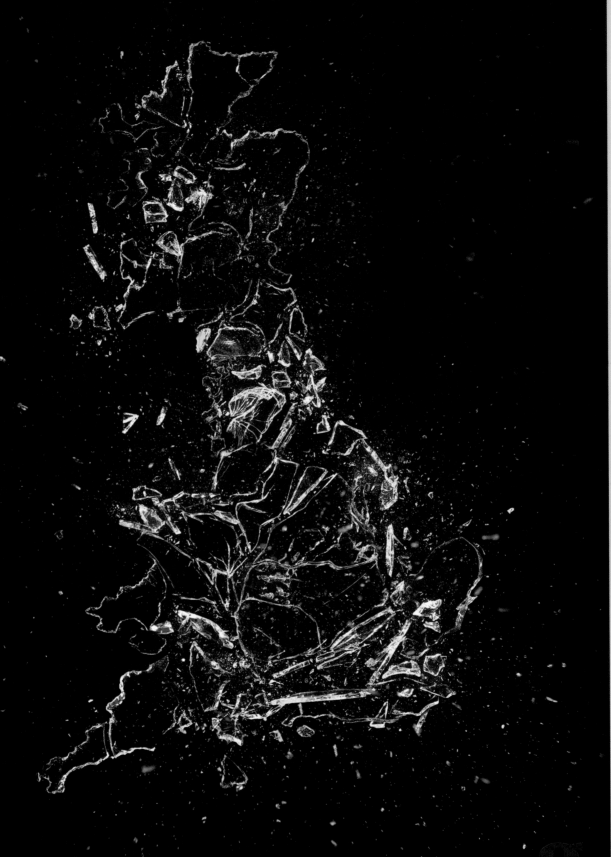

theguardian

Reading the Riots: a six day investigation
Starting on Monday in the Guardian
guardian.co.uk/readingtheriots

Advertising Agency: Bailey Lauerman   **Creative Director:** John Hayden   **Design Director:** James Strange

Writers: John Hayden, Dan Roettger   **Retoucher:** Joe McDermott   **Client:** Bass Pro Shops

ASSIGNMENT

Create a series of posters to introduce a new brand at the 2012 SHOT Show. The SHOT Show is the world's premier hunting and shooting trade show, attracting buyers and enthusiasts from more than 100 countries.

APPROACH

We wanted the design and placement of the product to reflect the care and precision that went into creating them. The tone and humor of the ads connect the brand emotionally to hunters and shooters.

RESULTS

The introduction generated a high degree of interest within the industry, and positioned Oculus as the next big idea in hunting optics.

EVERYTHING IS NOW POINT-BLANK RANGE.

SCOPES & BINOCULARS

OCULUS

Advertising Agencies beacon communications k.k. and Leo Burnett Tokyo   **Art Directors:** Yusuke Morotomi, Yukichi Shikata

Creative Directors: Yongbom Seo, Taketo Igarashi   **Copywriter:** Taketo Igarashi

Executive Creative Director: Jon King   **Designers:** Kiyoshi Honda, Fumio Tanaka, Hiroki Imatake   **Client:** Parrot S.A.

ASSIGNMENT

The AR Drone is the world's first WiFi controlled quadricopter piloted by multi-touch on a Smartphone. We simply needed to get people to feel the fun of this unreal innovation.

APPROACH

We developed a banner ad that lets consumers actually experience what it feels like to "control a drone with a Smartphone."

RESULTS

Awareness of the AR Drone soared. We achieved five times more than standard click through levels on livedoor. jp, one of the Japan's major news portal sites—livedoor. jp daily average PV is 1.5 million.

The Flying Banner

Advertising Agency: MacLaren McCann Calgary   **Art Director and Creative Director:** Mike Meadus   **Client:** Grumans Deli

ASSIGNMENT

We wanted to show that Grumans was delicious. And Jewish.

APPROACH

We wanted to be simple with our messaging. By using the Stars of David to play off a 5-star restaurant review, we get our message out in the simplest way possible.

RESULTS

Good luck getting a table.

" ✡ ✡ ✡ ✡ ✡ "

GRUMANS DELICATESSEN   230 11TH AVE SE   GRUMANS.CA

Advertising Agencies: Pentagram Design and Tishman Speyer

Designers: Matt McInerney, Kelly Sung

Art Director: Michael Gericke

Client: Tishman Speyer

Advertising Agencies: Pentagram Design and Tishman Speyer

Designers: Matt McInerney, Kelly Sung

Art Director: Michael Gericke

Client: Tishman Speyer

RESTAURANT DAYS
AT ROCKEFELLER CENTER®

PICNIC IN
THE PLAZA
MAY 16–18
11AM – 2PM

FOR DETAILS 212.632.3975

ROCKEFELLERCENTER.COM

Advertising Agency: DeVito/Verdi   **Art Director:** Manny Santos   **Creative Director:** Sal DeVito

Copywriters: Barry Flanik, Eric Schutte   **Agency Producer:** John Doepp   **Client:** Legal Sea Foods

ASSIGNMENT

Our assignment with this campaign was to let consumers know that Legal Sea Foods serves only the freshest fish and seafood available. At the same time, we are also making consumers aware of the company's unparalleled commitment to sustainable fishing practices.

APPROACH

In order to maximize our marketing budget, we decided to generate buzz with a series of PSA-style print ads (and accompanying TV spots) that delivered our message of fresh seafood while also provoking discussion about sustainable fishing.

RESULTS

Legal Sea Foods is a privately-held company, and thus chooses not to reveal business results publicly; however, this campaign generated a massive amount of publicity for the company, including articles in *USA Today* and other newspapers across the nation; broadcasts on national TV and radio programs; and numerous mentions from bloggers and other Internet sources. Client reaction was overwhelmingly positive. The national response proved we were able to leverage our marketing dollars to maximum effect.

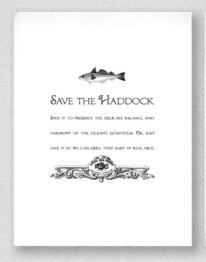
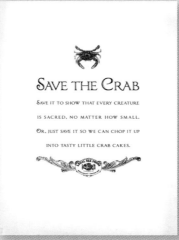

SAVE THE HADDOCK

SAVE IT TO PRESERVE THE DELICATE BALANCE AND

HARMONY OF THE OCEAN'S ECOSYSTEM. OR, JUST

SAVE IT SO WE CAN GRILL THAT BABY UP REAL NICE.

SAVE THE CRAB

SAVE IT TO SHOW THAT EVERY CREATURE

IS SACRED, NO MATTER HOW SMALL.

OR, JUST SAVE IT SO WE CAN CHOP IT UP

INTO TASTY LITTLE CRAB CAKES.

SAVE THE SALMON

SAVE IT SO OUR CHILDREN CAN WITNESS THE

GRACE AND BEAUTY OF THIS NOBLE FISH.

OR, JUST SAVE IT SO WE CAN SAUTÉ IT WITH

OUR FABULOUS LEMON CHIVE BUTTER SAUCE.

Advertising Agency: Target inHouse   **Art Director:** Kelsey Ciatti-Miller   **Creative Directors:** Cathe Jacobi and David Slack

Copywriters: Anna Stassen, Kiera Jacobson   **Producers:** Jodi Heller, Kathy Lally

Account Executive: Laura Ventrella   **Art Buyer:** Erin Repesh   **Production:** Heather Kern

Animators: Pixel Farm   **Client:** Target up&up brand

ASSIGNMENT

Create an awareness campaign for the wide product assortment of Target's owned brand, up&up.

APPROACH

The "Making Life Complete" campaign showcases the brand's breadth of assortment by highlighting specific categories and key products found throughout the store. Ultimately, it turns everyday products into beautiful, artful icons.

RESULTS

The clients and the up&up merchants were thrilled to see so many products in a single advertisement. They found the image arresting, and felt confident that our guests would be inspired to look for more up&up when they are in the store and may even be surprised by the assortment. They were so excited about the first four ads, they asked us to do a special version for up&up summer products, as well as five correlating online videos.

Mother's mighty, affordable little helpers.

Over 1,000 quality products you can't live without, at prices you can happily live with. Find online savings at coupons.target.com/upup-coupons.

only at

Advertising Agency: DeVito/Verdi   **Art Directors:** Brad Emmett, Sherrod Melvin, Chris Turner   **Creative Director:** Brad Emmett

Agency Producer: John Doepp   **Copywriters:** Brad Emmett, John DeVito, Chris Turner

Photographer: Nino Muñoz   **Client:** Daffy's

ASSIGNMENT

Daffy's is an off-price retailer in New York, selling designer clothes for significantly less than department stores. While the chain has always received high marks for its low prices, its perception as a place that sells fashion merchandise has suffered. Our task was to highlight Daffy's collection of fashion merchandise, while reinforcing its low-price position.

APPROACH

We created a campaign with models and images that playfully spoofed typical fashion advertising. With poses that looked like they were ripped from the pages of *Vogue*, our models were dressed in designer fashions, but always with a surprising twist—most notably, the low price of the garment.

RESULTS

During the period the campaign ran, sales of Daffy's fashion merchandise increased by double digits.

What's even more absurd is that her $110 dress is only $29.99.
DAFFY'S
daffys.com

Advertising Agency: MacLaren McCann Calgary   **Creative Director:** Mike Meadus   **Art Director:** Alex van der Breggen

Copywriter: Sean Mitchell   **Client:** Knifewear

ASSIGNMENT

The client wanted to show the level of control, precision, and creativity gained through cooking with exceptionally sharp, hand-forged Japanese kitchen knives.

APPROACH

The true test of a knife is how thinly it slices. When Knifewear showed us how their Japanese knives can go beyond paper-thin slicing, we knew origami was the perfect solution to show the transformation of raw food into culinary art.

RESULTS

Results included a spike in local sales, Internet orders from as far away as Australia, and a growing notoriety that nothing in the western world even comes close to Knifewear for traditional Japanese steel.

·KNIFEWEAR·

PRECISION JAPANESE CUTLERY

Advertising Agency: The 2M Group, Inc.   **Creative Director:** Meg Goodman   **Client:** Neiman Marcus

ASSIGNMENT

The client wanted to present an elegant visual that said "spring" in a powerful, yet elegant way. Initially, they thought they wanted to shoot an ethereal fashion-oriented image, but when TOGASHI showed his many dynamic, graphic, and elegant botanical photographs that were available for licensing, they quickly and eagerly selected this iconic cherry blossom shot.

RESULTS

The results speak for themselves. The agency designed a stunning piece and the client was extremely pleased.

BROADWAY PLAZA

PROUDLY WELCOMING NEIMAN MARCUS *March 9th*

Advertising Agency: Colle+McVoy   **Art Director:** Mike Caguin   **Writers:** Mike Caguin, Eric Husband

Client: Colle+McVoy

ASSIGNMENT

We created an ad for the agency to run in the Advertising Week conference program guide.

APPROACH

We aimed to be more entertaining and relevant with an idea that recognizes the different personalities you often find at industry events like Advertising Week. The networker. The social media "expert." The chronic Tweeter. We used these attendees, and the fodder that accompanies, to create a game of bingo.

RESULTS

The folks at Advertising Week liked the concept so well that they gave us prime placement in the program. During the conference, we caught several people chuckling while reading our ad—and maybe laughing, just maybe, at themselves.

Advertising Week

BINGO

Brooding exec in all black	Person seeking phone charger	Stuart Elliott sighting	Name-dropper	Copious note taker
Photo op seeker	QR code crusader	SEO/SEM confusion	Serial tweeter	"Advertising is dead" declaration
First in line every time	Personal space violator	**FREE DRINK**	Self-proclaimed social media expert	Matt Scheckner on his phone
Provocative panelist	Change agent looking to change jobs	Person unimpressed with everything	"Flushed out" for "Fleshed out"	Inspiring speaker
Extra-firm handshaker	Someone falling asleep (and snoring)	"Ecosystem" and "integrated" in one sentence	Overstuffed bag of swag	Attendee not yet on Facebook

May you experience all of the fun that makes Advertising Week, Advertising Week.

COLLE + McVOY

collemcvoy.com

Advertising Agency: Colle+McVoy   **Chief Creative Officer:** Mike Caguin   **Executive Creative Director:** Eric Husband

Writers: Chris Gault, John Neerland, Joel Stacy, Ryan Burk   **Art Director:** Mike Caguin

Photographer: Chris Peters   **Retoucher:** Greg Goranson   **Production Artist:** Jim Finnegan   **Client:** Colle+McVoy

ASSIGNMENT

Figure out a way to get better, more timely completion of timesheets throughout the agency.

APPROACH

Gently tar and feather the worst offenders by featuring them on oversized posters designed to offer pithy wisdom about the benefits of actually doing your timesheets.

RESULTS

Participation sky-rocketed during the first month, but it remains an ongoing battle. We are dealing with ADD agency folk, after all.

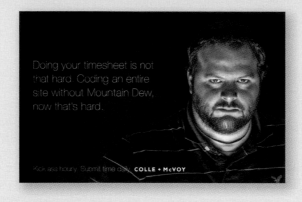

I believe in two things.
Doing my timesheet every day.
And Dungeons & Dragons.

Kick ass hourly. Submit time daily. **COLLE + McVOY**

Don't hate me
because I'm billable.

Kick ass hourly. Submit time daily. **COLLE + McVOY**

Advertising Agency: STUDIO INTERNATIONAL   **Creative Director and Designer:** Boris Ljubicic   **Client:** Croatian Football Federation

ASSIGNMENT

The assignment was a poster for the EURO 2012 sixteen national football teams (commissioned by Poland-Ukraine). The poster should represent EURO 2012 as a unique sport competition of sixteen national teams. Special emphasis should be placed on the Croatian National Team, which should be highlighted, but it shouldn't be bigger than the other nations, because the poster would be distributed to all national teams.

APPROACH

This design is a combination of national colors and typography, which are extracted numbers from the backs of football players' jerseys. The order of the numbers alternates by rows: at first they go from right to the left, then next, from left to the right, which represents a certain movement. All sixteen national teams (numbers) are illustrated by a photo in which the jersey numbers appear just as they do in real active game play on the field—wet, sunlit, crumpled, and lively. The Croatian sports jersey is under number "8" and it is highlighted with a square grid of red and white fields.

RESULTS

The poster was acceptable to all because every national team was involved in it with their visual identity. Croatian Football Federation shared the poster on EURO 2012, as their public relations and sport fair-play contribution to the championship. The poster was well accepted by football fans in Europe, and it was awarded by several international competitions.

Advertising Agency: Goodby, Silverstein & Partners

Executive Creative Director: Rick Dennis

Producer: Sheila Settles

Chief Creative Officers: Jeff Goodby, Rich Silverstein

Associate Creative Director: Michael Corbeille

Client: Goodby, Silverstein & Partners

216 SELF-PROMOTION GOLD DETROIT - SAN FRANCISCO BRIDGE

Advertising Agency: Goodby, Silverstein & Partners

Executive Creative Director: Rick Dennis

Producer: Sheila Settles

Chief Creative Officers: Jeff Goodby, Rich Silverstein

Associate Creative Director: Michael Corbeille

Client: Goodby, Silverstein & Partners

SAN FRANCISCO | DETROIT

Advertising Agency: Hub Strategy

Creative Directors: DJ O'Neil, Peter Judd

Copywriter: Chris Elzinga

Associate Creative Director: Jason Rothman

Designer: Jason Rothman

Client: Oakland A's

ASSIGNMENT

The premise for the "Green Collar Baseball" campaign stemmed from the lively spirit, hard-working attitude, and deep-rooted love that A's have for the game. Unlike most other MLB teams that are loaded with big name players and big time contracts, the A's are known for raising and creating amazing young talent that eventually turn into superstars. What they lack in experience, they make up for with an extra measure of effort, creativity, and fun—playing baseball the way it was meant to be played—full of hustle and passion. After a great response from the fans and players in 2010, we revisited the concept of "Green Collar Baseball" for the 2011 Oakland A's season.

APPROACH

We started with headlines that were consistent with the smart, no-nonsense tone of Green Collar Baseball. Next, we assembled the look and feel for the campaign by photographing a custom, handwritten typeface and grimed-up athletic tape for the headlines. We then layered the headlines on top of raging A's still footage. The resulting compositions gave us the gritty, unadulterated baseball feel the young team was looking for.

RESULTS

As a result of our "Green Collar Baseball" campaign, the A's sold almost 60,000 more single game tickets than the previous year. We received great feedback from A's fans (and even Giants' fans) from all over the Bay area, as well as recognition from The National Sports Forum ADchievement Awards—the only national, all-encompassing awards program honoring advertising from throughout the sports industry—who awarded us Best Television campaign, Best Social/Mobile media campaign, and third place in the Out-of-Home category. The A's considered this a huge success, as it was the best placing their advertising has ever received. The client was so happy with the results they decided to continue the "Green Collar Baseball" campaign for a third year, into the 2012 season, with a revamped look and feel. Currently the A's are shaking up the MLB and fighting for the wild card playoff bid, despite payroll differences of over 90 million dollars on their competition. We like to think our "Green Collar Baseball" campaign had a little something to do with it.

WE PICK OUR BATTLES.

ALL 162 OF THEM.

GREEN COLLAR BASEBALL

PROFESSIONAL STUNTS.
DO NOT ATTEMPT.

WE WORK HARD AT MAKING IT LOOK EASY.

OAKLANDATHLETICS.COM

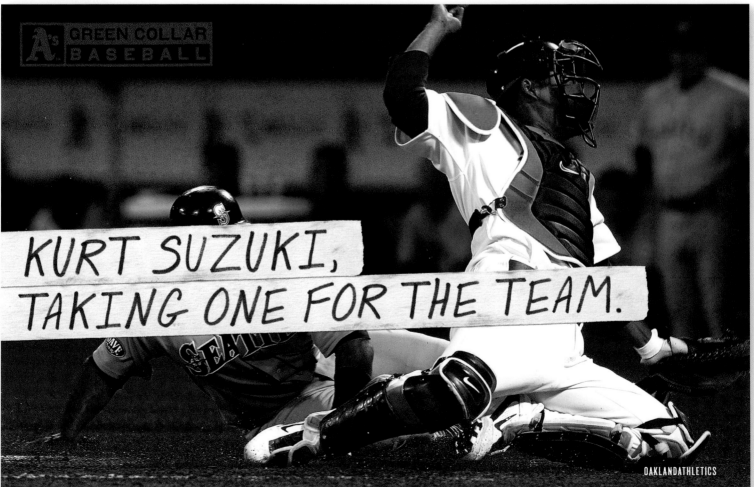

KURT SUZUKI, TAKING ONE FOR THE TEAM.

OAKLANDATHLETICS

Advertising Agency: jotabequ GREY   **Art Director:** Héctor Acuña   **Creative Director:** Alexander Obando

Designer: Pablo Salazar   **Client:** Gold's Gym Costa Rica

ASSIGNMENT

Our goal was to create a group of pieces that clearly communicate one of the main benefits of being in a gym—strengthening your body—but make it different from all of the other, more traditional, gym communications in our country.

APPROACH

A strong body is a common benefit that any gym can offer and can be communicated in many ways, so the challenge we faced was to clearly communicate that message without using common elements or persons exercising in a gym.

RESULTS

The client was very satisfied with the proposal. The images are used in advertisements in local newspapers and as motivational posters in the gym.

Advertising Agency: Factory Design Labs

Creative Director: Emily Philpott

Art Buyer: Jill Groves

Associate Creative Directors: Josh Wills, Bryan Cavanagh, Tom Goodrich

Senior Art Director: Kris Fry

Art Director: Steve Hurd

Client: Oakley Inc.

ASSIGNMENT

Factory came to me in 2011 with a project to capture Oakley-sponsored athletes in their preparation for the 2012 London Olympic Games. Sports, athletes, and, in particular, the Olympics have been the backbone of my career. The concept was to illustrate the one, singularly persuasive idea that athletes choose Oakley as their eyewear—going "Beyond Reason"—to place themselves at the start line of their chosen sports.

APPROACH

We traveled extensively to visit these athletes-in-training at their home venues. The idea was to capture as closely as possible a training day, so to respond to the rigors and dedication they go through every day when no one is watching. I shot reportage-style for some of the day, while they were doing their workouts, but also re-created moments that had inspired me from training or my experience around the sport. I didn't want to over-engineer the images. The work that the creatives from Factory responded to had an editorial feel to it, but because I had shot a couple of photo books over the last couple of years, it was classic press work. I mostly shot everything with a very wide aperture to focus the eye on the athlete and the eyewear, which is right where the point of focus was. This allowed the background to drop off and be soft. A very subtle amount of lighting was used throughout. We encountered the craziest weather during the whole trip—a drenching California rainstorm with fog and black storm clouds over Oscar Pistorious's track, and snow in Palma, Spain (for the first time in fifty years). This played into our favor and didn't disrupt the tight shooting schedule, but instead added a lot more drama and mood to the images.

RESULTS

From what I understand, all were very happy.

BEYOND REASON™

I AM DRIVEN BY THE FEAR THAT SOMEONE ELSE IS TRAINING JUST A LITTLE BIT HARDER THAN ME | BRYAN CLAY

BEYOND REASON™

THE ONLY DIFFERENCE BETWEEN MY BROTHER AND ME IS THAT HE PUTS HIS SHOES ON IN THE MORNING AND I PUT MY LEGS ON. AND I'M FASTER | OSCAR PISTORIUS

Advertising Agency: Colle+McVoy   **Executive Creative Director:** Mike Caguin   **Copywriter:** Joel Stacy

Art Director: Matt Pruett   **Creative Director:** Brian Ritchie   **Client:** Cannondale Bicycle Corporation

ASSIGNMENT

Our objective was to create a compelling print ad that highlighted the technology and innovation behind Cannondale's new SuperSix Evo road bike while, most importantly, illustrating the benefit to consumers.

APPROACH

We wanted the ad to be a reflection of the bike itself. Clean. Concise. And purposeful.

RESULTS

Our client loved the look, feel, and tone of the ad. So much so, that they ended up using the headline in other pieces of creative.

cannondale

OUT CORNER. OUT CLIMB.
OUT SPRINT. OUT EVERYTHING.

At **695 GRAMS,** lightness is only part of what makes the **2012 SUPERSIX EVO** the fastest race bike ever created. Designed to be more aerodynamic, and more compliant, it also recorded the best stiffness-to-weight ratio ever — **142.3 NM/DEG/KG**. Add it all up, and you have the perfect ride.

createtheperfectride.com

Advertising Agency: MRM/McCann - Salt Lake   **Executive Creative Director:** Brian Deaver   **Photographer:** Josh Wood

Associate Creative Directors: Joe Bartenhagen, Terry Urruty   **Client:** Salt Lake Film Society

ASSIGNMENT

The Salt Lake Film Society shows classic and independent films. They were looking for ways to create awareness around membership benefits.

APPROACH

We created a series of lobby posters that focused on the thing we loved most about these theaters—their profound sense of character.

RESULTS

The campaign is still fresh and results are pending.

Our seats don't recline. But they do occasionally give out.

Tower Theater SLFS
3:00 PM Tue 5/15/12
AD1MAT $6.25
PG13
1

Join the Salt Lake Film Society and help make our theaters as special as the movies we show.

SLFS
salt lake film society

We don't have assigned seating. But we do have a velvet rope.

Tower Theater SLFS
8:20 PM Sat 4/21/12
AD1EVE $8.75
R
1

Join the Salt Lake Film Society and help make our theaters as special as the movies we show.

SLFS
salt lake film society

Advertising Agency: Peter Mayer Advertising   **Creative Director:** Neil Landry   **Graphic Designer:** Momko Kimura

Copywriter: Lori Archer-Smith   **Client:** Louisiana Department of Culture, Recreation & Tourism

ASSIGNMENT

The agency was tasked with promoting Louisiana as a vacation destination.

APPROACH

Our approach was to show that Louisiana has something for everyone.

Searching for a dozen oysters, salty and cold.

Getting off the beaten path.

Satisfying a different appetite.

LOU!S!ANA
Pick your Passion™
LouisianaTravel.com

© 2011 The Louisiana Department of Culture, Recreation & Tourism

This is my *Louisiana.*

Terrance Simien

Terrance Simien,
Zydeco Cajun Grammy Award Winner
Louisiana Native

"You don't need a radio to hear our music. You need a map. We have great festivals all over the state. Come for the food, dancin', more food, more dancin'."

To see what other Louisiana insiders recommend and to create your own Louisiana tour, visit LouisianaTravel.com or call 1-800-99-GUMBO.

Kisatchie National Forest
Opelousas
Henderson
Covington

LOUISIANA
OFFICE OF THE LT. GOVERNOR
Department of Culture, Recreation & Tourism

Advertising Agency: BVK   **Creative Directors:** Mitch Markussen, Nick Pipitone, Rich Kohnke, Ross Lowinske   **Client:** Maine Office of Tourism

ASSIGNMENT

To create a campaign promoting tourism in Maine, highlighting actual residents of Maine (called the "insiders"). Make the message authentic, homegrown, and pure—and highlight what makes Maine an extremely unique place to visit.

APPROACH

First, we had to identify "insiders" that fit into certain categories—outdoor/hiking, beach/surfing, culture, farm to table, etc. Once we identified the people, we got their story and built the work around that, giving the state a one-of-a-kind approachability and charm.

RESULTS

As of this date, request for Maine Visitors Guides have increased 17.6% over last year.

Honey, sell the FURNITURE, we need to MAKE ROOM FOR the kayaks.

BRONWYN, Fresh air-aholic

Maine is about as far north and east as you can get. And we're the first state to see the sunrise everyday. Here, there are one-of-a-kind adventures around every corner, including the easternmost national park in the U.S., Acadia National Park. So get outside and find your Maine Thing. Get the unfiltered story at **VisitMaine.com**.

Advertising Agency: MHC STUDIO   **Creative Director:** William Taylor   **Senior Designer:** Jason Scuderi   **Client:** Sweets

ASSIGNMENT

Since 1906 Sweets has been the premier resource for architectural building products, so—as the natural progression goes—they developed an online version in 1992 and an app this year to augment their online search and download capabilities. Our assignment was to introduce the Sweets app and its capabilities.

APPROACH

The Sweets app is a deep resource for searching building products, browsing Masterformat categories, and finding downloadable digital files for architectural plans and specifications We took this very functional app and presented it as an architect would present a building plan by using 3d rendering to show the various layers of the app, and detailed information aligned with the layer.

RESULTS

There have been over 9,000 downloads of the Sweets app. Between March 2011 and March 2012, Sweets experienced a 44% increase in new contracts from building product manufacturers. Overall, content contributed by new and existing building product manufacturers increased by 48%. During this same period, Sweets.com registered users grew by 43% and content downloads increased by 44%.

Introducing the Sweets Mobile App

Download the Sweets Building Products App at the iTunes Store or Google Play.

Advertising Agency: MHC STUDIO

Creative Director: William Taylor

Senior Designer: Jason Scuderi

Intern: Chelsea Hunter

Design Firm: Bryan Christie Design

Illustrator: Jeong Suh

Client: Sweets

ASSIGNMENT

In 1906, Sweets Catalog File was introduced to the architectural community and subsequently became the premier resource for architects to find building products. When Sweets moved its information online, it faced the challenge of managing the transition of revenue from a yearly print business to a competitive digital media offering where building product information could be updated more frequently. Key to that transition was user marketing that drove qualified construction professionals (architects, engineers, contractors, etc.) to engage with a brand with which they were familiar, but now in a different medium. Our assignment was to reposition Sweets as the digital destination of choice to find building products and download valuable supporting material that is required to incorporate products into architectural plans. Architects and Specifiers are information gatherers and are drawn to detailed information about products and how they are put in place in buildings they admire. The print advertising campaign played to their personalities by featuring celebrated buildings with detailed information on building products found in Sweets.com. We prominently placed the iconic Sweets logo and used green dots, in the same proportion and color as the logo, to call out the building products. Architects and Specifiers were drawn to the information they crave, and building product manufacturers were motivated to be a part of this engaging conversation by listing their products in Sweets.

RESULTS

Shortly after the print campaign ran in *Architectural Record*, the Sales team received unsolicited calls from building product manufacturers to be part of Sweets.com. Between March 2011 and March 2012, Sweets experienced a 44% increase in new contracts from building product manufacturers. Overall, content contributed by new and existing building product manufacturers increased by 48%. During this same period, Sweets.com registered users grew by 43% and content downloads increased by 44%. Page views per visit also increased by 56%.

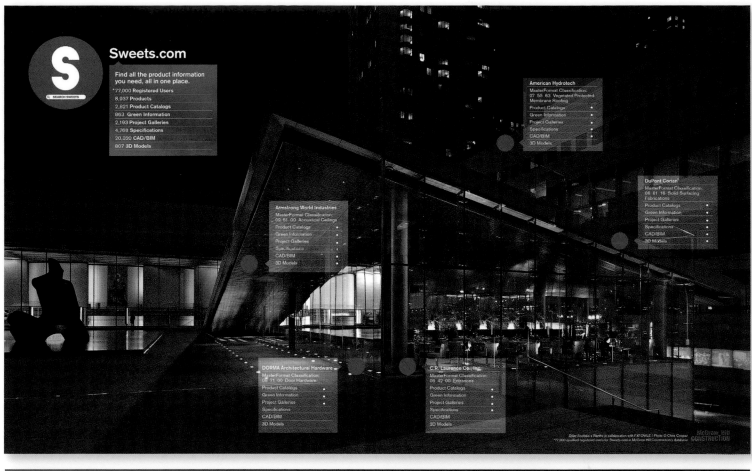

Advertising Agency: Peter Mayer Advertising **Graphic Designer:** Jesse Gresham **Creative Director:** Joel Mody

Copywriter: Maureen Bongiovanni **Client:** Mississippi Power

ASSIGNMENT

Agency was tasked advertise Mississippi Power.

APPROACH

Our approach was to show how Mississippi Power cared for and affected a variety of peoples' lives.

then

now

POWERING WHAT'S NEXT.

Who would've thought we'd ever be plugging in books, booting up classrooms, or logging into newspapers? The fact is, today's average American uses about twice as much electricity as he did in the 1970s. So to keep up, Mississippi Power is investing in new technology, new facilities and more efficient power grids to ensure we can meet tomorrow's energy needs, no matter what tomorrow brings. Mississippi Power. Powering what's next.

CANADA

WAX | Calgary Farmers' Market

MacLaren McCann Calgary | Knifewear

CANADA

COSTA RICA

rhed | rhed

Jotabequ GREY | Gold's Gym Costa Rica

Goodby, Silverstein & Partners | Golden Gate National Parks Conservancy

Bailey Lauerman | Cargill

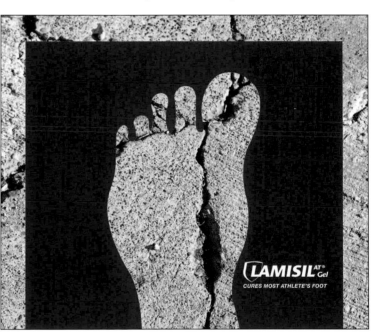

Leo Burnett Warsaw | Procter & Gamble

Saatchi & Saatchi | Novartis Lamisil

The Gate Worldwide | State Street Global Advisors

Lloyd & Company | Bottega Veneta

Butler, Shine, Stern & Partners | Sorel

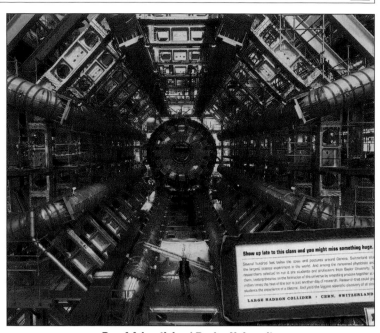

Proof Advertising | Baylor University

Innocean Worldwide Americas | Hyundai

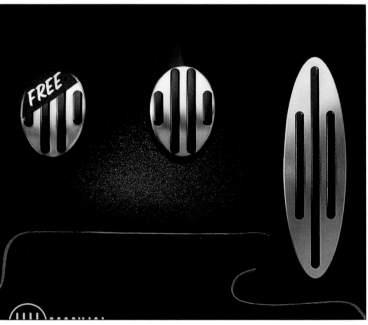

Butler, Shine, Stern & Partners | MINI USA

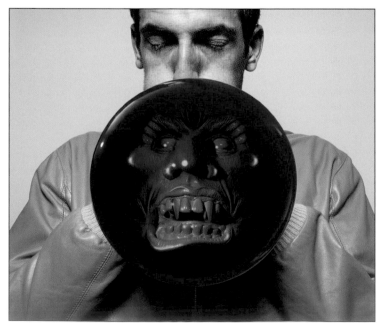

Publicis New York | P&G/Scope

HOOK | Charleston Mix

mcgarrybowen | Motorola

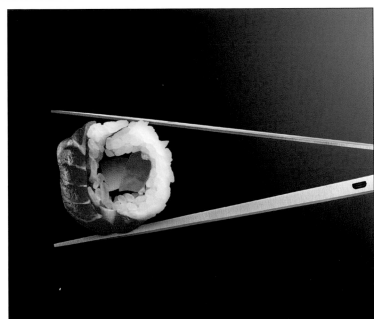

MRM / McCann Salt Lake City | Intel

Hub Strategy & Communications | Oakland A's

Dunn&Co. | Florida Department of Transportation

DeVito/Verdi | Daffy's

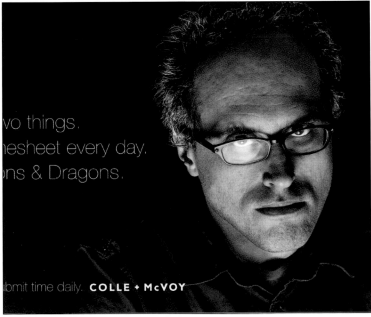

Colle+McVoy | Colle+McVoy

BEST IN AMERICAS

CANADA

Hawk Marketing Services   MacLaren McCann Calgary   WAX   rhed

USA

Colle + McVoy	Saatchi & Saatchi LA	Butler, Shine, Stern & Partners	PP+K	14-Forty	Innocean Worldwide Americas
TBWA Chiat Day	The Gate Worldwide	Greenfield/Belser	Pennebaker	Hub Strategy	Doe Anderson
Sargent & Berman	MiresBall	The Refinery	Alcone Marketing	Freelance	YARD
HOOK	Pentagram Design	Mutual of Omaha	hawkeye	The Richards Group	Dunn&Co.
MRM/McCann	Schatz Ornstein Studio	BVK	Michael Schwab Studio	Saatchi & Saatchi, New York	McGraw-Hill Construction
chadvertising	McGraw-Hill Construction	Peter Mayer Advertising	Bailey Lauerman	Goodby, Silverstein & Partners	DeVito/Verdi
Brick Design	Communica, Inc.	Fox Chase Cancer Center	The Great Society	JWT Germany	Jude Buffum Illustration + Design
Target Corporation	White & Case LLP	John McNeil Studio	mike powell photography	Publicis New York	
Imaginary Lines	GSD&M	Kiyoshi TOGASHI Photography	BBDO Proximity Minne160over90	Sandro Inc.	
Christopher Griffith Studio	gallop studio		LLOYD&CO	Struck	
Proof Advertising					

COSTA RICA

Jotabequ GREY

CROATIA

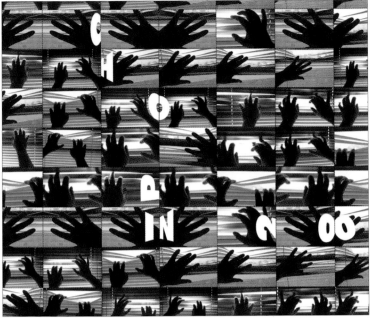

STUDIO INTERNATIONAL | Croatian Football Federation

STUDIO INTERNATIONAL | Clavis - Music Teachers Association

GERMANY

UNITED KINGDOM

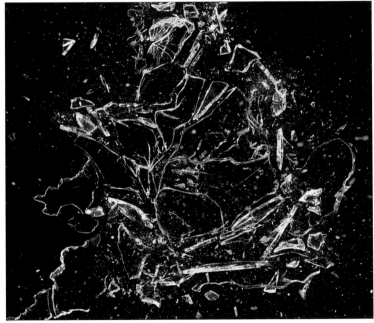

Schneider/Waibel | d&b audiotechnik GmbH

Wieden & Kennedy | The Guardian

DUBAI

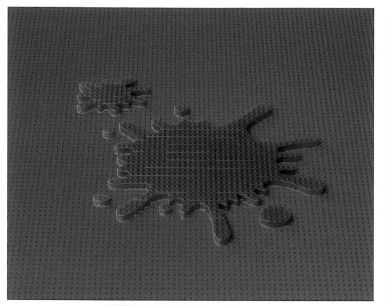

DDB Dubai, UAE | Clorox Company

JAPAN

H-57 Creative Station | FirstFloorUnder.com

THAILAND

Your wife won't even know you're gone!

PRIUS
The New Toyota Prius
The quietest car on earth.

Charit Art Co., Ltd. | Toyota Motor Thailand Co.,Ltd.

PARKISTAN

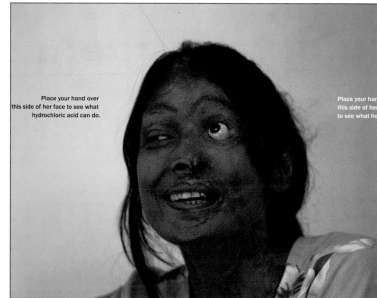

Place your hand over this side of her face to see what hydrochloric acid can do.

Place your han this side of her to see what ho

IAL Saatchi & Saatchi Pakistan | Depilex Smile Again Foundation

BEST IN EUROPE & AFRICA

CROATIA

STUDIO INTERNATIONAL

GERMANY

Waibel Werbeagentur

HUNGARY

Republic Group

UNITED KINGDOM

Jonathan Knowles Photography

RUSSIAN FEDERATION

ADDICT communications

BEST IN ASIA & OCEANIA

JAPAN

beacon communications k.k.   oguma graphic   omdr design agency

PAKISTAN

IAL Saatchi & Saatchi

THAILAND

Charit Art Co., Ltd.

DUBAI

DDB DUBAI   UAE

14-Forty
www.14-forty.com
2335 Hyperion Ave.
Los Angeles, CA 90027, United States
Tel 323 662 1440 | Fax 323 668 2037

160over90
www.160over90.com
1 South Broad
Philadelphia, PA 19107, United States
Tel 215 732 3200 | Fax 215 732 1664

Bailey Lauerman
www.baileylauerman.com
1248 O St., Suite 900
Lincoln, NE 68508, United States
Tel 402 475 2800 | Fax 402 475 5115

BBDO Proximity Minneapolis
www.bbdo.com
150 South 5th Street, Suite 3500
Minneapolis, MN 55402, United States
Tel 612 338 8401 | Fax 612 656 0602

beacon communications k.k.
www.beaconcom.jp
JR Tokyu Meguro Building
Tokyo, 141-0021, Japan
Tel 813 5437 7450

Butler, Shine, Stern & Partners
www.bssp.com
20 Liberty Ship Way
Sausalito, CA 94965, United States
Tel 415 944 8279

bvk
www.bvk.com
250 West Coventry Court, Suite 300
Milwaukee, WI 53217, United States
Tel 414 228 1990

Chadvertising
www.chadvertising.com
130 Arizona Ave., #417
Atlanta, GA 30307, United States
Tel 469 222 8729

Charit Art Co., Ltd.
415/1 Ladprao 107 Bangkapi
Bangkok 10240, Thailand
Tel (66)81 642 3922

Communica, Inc.
www.communica-usa.com
31 North Erie Stree
Toledo, OH 43604, United States
Tel 800 800 7890 | Fax 888 445 7765

DDB Dubai
www.ddb.ae
DDB FZ LLC
PO Box 71996, #21
Dubai Media City
Dubai, UAE
Tel +971 4 429 0904 | Fax +971 4 429 0903

DeVito/Verdi
www.devitoverdi.com
100 5th Avenue, 16th Floor
New York, NY 10011, United States
Tel 212 431 4694 | Fax 212 431 4940

Doe Anderson
www.doeanderson.com
620 West Main St.
Louisville, KY 40202, United States
Tel 502 815 3272

Dunn&Co.
www.dunn-co.com
202 S. 22nd St., Ste. 202
Tampa, FL 33605, United States
Tel 813 350 7990

gallop studio
www.gallop.com
2500 Broadway Street N.E.
Minneapolis, MN 55413, United States
Tel 612 379 8040

Goodby, Silverstein & Partners
www.goodbysilverstein.com
720 California Street
San Francisco, CA 94108, United States
Tel 415 955 5683

GSD&M
www.gsdm.com
828 West 6th Street
Austin, TX 78703, United States
Tel 512 242 4736

Havas Worldwide Bangkok Co., Ltd.
www.havasworldwide.com
29 Bangkok Business Center Building, 28th
Floor, Room 2802
Soi Ekamai Sukhumvit 63 Klongton Nua
Wattana Bangkok 10110 Thailand
Tel +66 2 382 1722 | Fax +66 2 382 1727

Hawk Marketing Services
www.hawk.ca
28-77 Vaughan Harvey Blvd., 4th Floor
Moncton, New Brunswick E1C0K2 Canada
Tel 506 877 1400 | Fax 506 877 1501

HOOK
www.hookusa.com
409 King Street, Floor 4v
Charleston, SC 29403, United States
Tel 843 853 5532

Hub Strategy & Communication
www.hubstrategy.com
39 Mesa St., Suite 212
San Francisco, CA 94129, United States
Tel 415 561 4345 | Fax 415 771 5965

IAL Saatchi & Saatchi
www.ialideas.com
72-C, 13th Commercial St.
Phase II Ext. DHA
Karachi, Pakistan
Tel +9221 5312231-38 | Fax +9221 5897706

Imaginary Lines
imaginarylines.com
PO Box 176, 500 W. Nash
Terrell, TX 75160, United States
Tel 972 524 9055

Innocean Worldwide Americas
www.innoceanusa.com
180 5th Street, Suite 200
Huntington Beach, CA 92648, United States
Tel 714 861 5200 | Fax 714 861 5337

Jay Advertising
www.jayadvertising.com
170 Linden Oaks
Rochester, NY 14625, United States
Tel 585 264 3600 | Fax 585 264 3650

John McNeil Studio
johnmcneilstudio.com
720 Channing Street
Berkeley, CA 94710, United States
Tel 510 526 7100

Jonathan Knowles Photography
www.jknowles.com
48A Chancellors Road
London W6 9RS, United Kingdom
Tel +44 20 8741 7577

jotabequ GREY
www.jotabequ.com
Ruta 4 5-33, zona 4
Guatemala City n/a Guatemala
Tel +502 2416 4900 | Fax +502 2360 0059

Kiyoshi TOGASHI Photography
www.togashistudio.com
36 West 20 Street, 7th Floor
New York, NY 10011, United States
Tel 212 420 0206 | Fax 212 463 9073

Leo Burnett Warsaw
www.leoburnett.com
Platinum Business Park
Ul.Woloska 9 02-583 Warsaw, Poland
Tel +48 22 448 98 00

LLOYD & Company Advertising, Inc.
www.lloydandco.com
180 Varick Street, Suite 1018
New York, NY 10014, United States
Tel 212 414 3100 | Fax 212 414 3113

MacLaren McCann Calgary
www.maclaren.com
Suite 100-238 11 Ave. SE
Calgary AB T2G OX8, Canada
Tel 403 269 6120

McGraw-Hill Construction
61 Pierrepont Street, #43
Brooklyn, NY 11201, United States
Tel 917 439 6516

Michael Schwab Studio
www.michaelschwab.com
108 Tamalpais Avenue
San Anselmo, CA 94960, United States
Tel 415 257 5792

---

mike powell photography
www.mikepowellphoto.com
1284 Sandstone Way
Bellingham, WA 98229, United States
Tel 310 877 7940

MiresBall
www.miresball.com
2605 State Street
San Diego, CA 92103, United States
Tel 619 234 6631

MRM / McCann Salt Lake City
www.mccannslc.com
60 E. South Temple, Ste. 1400
Salt Lake City, UT 84111, United States
Tel 801 257 7700

omdr design agency
www.omdr.co.jp
107-0062 Unity 6-12-10 Minami-Aoyama
Minato-ku, Tokyo 202, Japan
Tel 03-5766-3410 | Fax 03-5766-3411

Pennebaker
www.pennebaker.com
1100 W. 23rd, Ste. 200
Houston, TX 77008, United States
Tel 713 963 8607 | Fax 713 960 9680

Pentagram Design
www.pentagram.com
204 Fifth Avenue
New York, NY 10010, United States
Tel 212 683 7000 | Fax 212 532 0181

Peter Mayer Advertising
www.peteramayer.com
318 Camp Street
New Orleans, LA 70130, United States
Tel 504 581 7191 | Fax 504 566 1046

pp+k
www.uniteppk.com
1102 North Florida Avenue
Tampa, FL 33602, United States
Tel 813 496 7000

Proof Advertising
www.proof-advertising.com
114 West 7th Street, Ste. 500
Austin, TX 78701, United States
Tel 512 345 6658 | Fax 512 345 6227

Publicis New York
www.publicis-usa.com
950 Sixth Avenue
New York, NY 10001, United States
Tel 212 279 5898

Republic Group
http://hellorepublic.com
Vigyazo Ferenc 4
Budapest 1051 Hungary
Tel +36 1 474 0023

rhed
477 Richmond St. W
Toronto ON, M5V3E7 Canada
Tel 416 504 5239

Saatchi & Saatchi, New York
www.saatchi.com
375 Hudson Street
New York, NY 10014 United States
Tel 212-463-3814 | Fax 212 463 9855

SAGA Advertising & Marketing
www.sagamarketing.com
570 Old Highway, 8 NW
New Brighton, MN 55112
Tel 651 287 0180 | Fax 651 287 0848

Sandro Inc.
2540 W. Huron St.
Chicago, IL 60612, United States
Tel 773 486 0300

Schatz Ornstein Studio
435 West Broadway, 2nd Floor
New York, NY 11211, United States
Tel 212 334 6667 | Fax 212 334 6669

Schneider/Waibel Werbeagentur
Neckarstrasse 237
D-70190 Stuttgart, Germany
Tel +49 711 9933 8000 | Fax +49 711 9933 8040

Serviceplan, Munich
www.serviceplan.com
Brienner Str 45 ad
80250 Munich, Germany
Tel +49 89 2050 20 | Fax +49 89 2050 2111

STIR
www.stirstuff.com
135 W. Wells St., Suite 800
Milwaukee, WI 53203, United States
Tel 414 278 0040

Struck Inc.
http://struck.com/
159 W. Broadway, Ste. 200
Salt Lake City, UT 84101, United States
Tel 801 531 0122

STUDIO INTERNATIONAL
www.studio-international.com
Buconjiceva 43
HR 10-000 Zagreb, Croatia
Tel 385 1 37 40 40 | Fax 385 1 37 08 320

Target Corporation
www.target.com
33 South Sixth Street CC-03
Minneapolis, MN 55402, United States
Tel 612 304 9858

TBWA/CHIAT/DAY
tbwachiatday.com
488 Madison Ave.
New York, NY 10022
Tel 212 804 1000 | Fax 212 804 1200

The Gate Worldwide
www.thegateworldwide.com
11 East 26th Street, 14th Floor
New York, NY 10022, United States
Tel 212 508 3400

WAX
www.wax.ca
320 333 24th Ave. SW
Calgary AB T2S 3E6, Canada
Tel 403 262 9323

YARD
www.yardnyc.com
130 W. 25TH St., 7th Floor
New York, NY 10001, United States
Tel 212 625 8372 | Fax 212 625 1460

mcgarrybowen
www.mcgarrybowen.com
601 West 26th Street
New York, NY 10001, United States
Tel 212 598 2900

Factory Design Labs
www.factorylabs.com
158 Filmore Street
Denver, CO 80206, United States
Tel 720 224 9518

Colle + McVoy
www.collemcvoy.com
400 First Avenue North, Suite 700
Minneapolis, MN 55401, United States
Tel 612 305 6169

The 2M Group, Inc.
www.the2mgroup.com
72A Main Street
Tiburon, CA 94920, United States
Tel 415 331 3331 | Fax 415 435 2708

Woodbine Agency
www.woodbine.com
210 Cherry Street S.
Winston-Salem, NC 27101, United States
Tel 336 724 0450

Syrup NYC
www.syrupnyc.com
12 Vestry Street, 7th Floor
New York, NY 10013, United States
Tel 212 680 1477

Hakuhodo, Inc.
www.hakuhodo.jp
Head Office
Akasaka Biz Tower, 5-3-1 Akasaka, Minato-ku,
Tokyo 107-6322, Japan
Tel +81-(0)3-6441-8111 (Reception)

Wieden & Kennedy
www.wk.com
150 Varick Street # 7
New York, NY 10013 , United States
Tel 917 661 5200

How to save on our Graphis Books

Standing Orders:

50% off or $60 for a $120 book, plus $10 for shipping & handling
Get our new books at our best deal, long before they arrive in book
stores! A Standing Order is a subscription commiment to the Graphis
books of your choice.

Standing Orders:

50% off or $60 for a $120 book, plus $10 for shipping & handling
Get our new books at our best deal, long before they arrive in book
stores! A Standing Order is a subscription commiment to the Graphis
books of your choice.

Graphis Titles

Poster Annual 2013

PLATINUM WINNERS:

Stephan Bundi
Atelier Bundi

Andrea Castelletti
Andrea Castelletti

Kuokwai Cheong
Cultural Affairs Bureau of the Macao S.A.R. Government

Hoon-Dong Chung
Dankook University

Fabrique
Fabrique

Toshiaki & Hisa Ide
IF Studio

AN Kiyoung
ANKiyoung Design Room

Michael Schwab
Michael Schwab Studio

Raymond Tam
A Green Hill Communications Limited

2013
Hardcover: 240 pages
200-plus color illustrations
Trim: 8.5 x 11.75"
ISBN: 1-931241-29-8
US $120

Graphis Poster 2013 is the definitive showcase of the 100 best Posters of the year chosen from numerous international entries. The collection features 9 Platinum and 91 Gold award-winning Posters from Italy, South Africa, Switzerland, Korea, The Netherlands, Japan and the United States, amongst many others. Graphis also features an interview with **Rick Valicenti**, the founder and Design Director of Thirst in Chicago — a firm devoted to "art, function and real human presence."

Advertising Annual 2013

Many a small thing has been made large by the right kind of advertising. ■ *Mark Twain, Author (1835-1910)*

2013
Hardcover: 256 pages
200-plus color images
Trim: 7 x 11 3/4"
ISBN: 1-932026-79-5
US $120

Graphis Advertising 2013 presents some of the top campaigns of the year selected from hundreds of entries. Featured are seasoned works from accomplished advertising agencies, such as **Goodby**, **Silverstein & Partners**, **Bailey Lauerman**, **BVK**, **DeVito/Verdi**, **HOOK**, and **Saatchi & Saatchi**. Each spread presents the work with a case study description written by each agency. These campaigns provide insight into the agency's creative process and how they met the needs of their clients.

Design Annual 2013

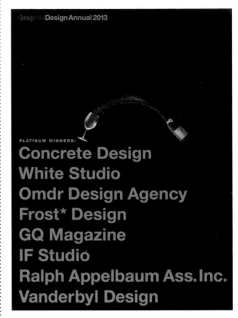

PLATINUM WINNERS:

Concrete Design
White Studio
Omdr Design Agency
Frost* Design
GQ Magazine
IF Studio
Ralph Appelbaum Ass. Inc.
Vanderbyl Design

2013
Hardcover: 256 pages
200-plus color images
Trim: 8.5 x 11.75"
ISBN: 1-932026-77-1
US $120

Graphis Design 2013 features the most compelling design work of the year selected from hundreds of international entries. This volume includes Platinum award – winning entries from **Alt Group**, **GQ Magazine**, **Turner Duckworth**, **Strømme Throndsen Design** and **White Studio**. All published entries are presented on a spread with a case study description written by each designer or design firm.

Branding 6

Graphis **Branding6**

8 EXCEPTIONAL BRANDING CASE STUDIES:

Pentagram
WAX
People Design
Cue
Firewood Inc.
The General Design
Studio International
Alt Group

2013
Hardcover: 256 pages
200-plus color images
Trim: 8.5 x 11.75"
ISBN: 1-932026-78-8
US $120

This book presents interviews, company profiles and visual histories of some of the biggest names in design and retail today, including: Q&A with **Pentagram**, **WAX**, **People design**, **Cue**, **Firewood**, **The General Design Co.**, **Studio International**, and **Alt Group**. All that, plus hundreds of images from the year's Graphis Gold Award-winning branding campaigns. This is a must-have for anyone interested in successful, creative branding – designers, businesses, students and fans alike.

Photography Annual 2013

2013
Hardcover: 256 pages
200-plus color images
Trim: 8.5 x 11.75"
ISBN:1-931241-80-1
US $120

Photography2013 is a moving collection of the years best photographs. Shot by some of the world's most respected photographers and selected from an international pool of entries, these beautifully reproduced images are organized by category for easy referencing. This year's book includes an interview with photographer **Bill Diadato**, discussing his background and the inspiration behind his work.

Masters of the 20th Century

MASTERS OF THE 20TH CENTURY
THE ICOGRADA DESIGN HALL OF FAME

CONCEIVED DESIGNED AND EDITED BY MERVYN KURLANSKY

2012
Hardcover: 360 pages
200-plus color illustrations
Trim: 10 x 12"
ISBN: 1-888001-85-2
US $70

This is a huge volume that features the work and biographies of more than 100 top designers worldwide. Designed and edited by **Mervyn Kurlansky**, with distinct profiles of **Pierre Bernard**, **Wolfgang Weingart** and many others. A testament to exceptional talents and proof that they'll be remembered for generations to come, this book comes complete with a companion CD-ROM containing hundreds of additional images. Forewards by **Steven Heller** and **Marion Wesel-Henrion**.